Wisdom With Understanding is Better Than Rubies

Lurine Karon Greenberg
Fine Arts Collection

AN AMERICAN ARCHITECTURE

FRANK LLOYD WRIGHT

EDITED BY EDGAR KAUFMANN

Pomegranate

SAN FRANCISCO

First published in 1955 by Horizon Press, Inc.

Published by Pomegranate Communications, Inc.
Box 808022, Petaluma CA 94975
800 227 1428; www.pomegranate.com

Pomegranate Europe Ltd.
Unit 1, Heathcote Business Centre
Hurlbutt Road, Warwick
Warwickshire CV34 6TD, UK
[+44] 0 1926 430111; sales@pomeurope.co.uk

2006 Pomegranate Communications, Inc.

ISBN 0-7649-3659-X
Pomegranate Catalog No. A108

Printed and bound in China

15 14 13 12 11 10 09 08 07 06   10 9 8 7 6 5 4 3 2 1

C O N T E N T S

ILLUSTRATIONS

COLOR ILLUSTRATIONS

EDITOR'S NOTE

Frank Lloyd Wright has won world-wide fame and admiration in more than sixty years devoted to "the mother art," architecture. But genius is inseparable from opposition: Mr. Wright's challenge to the accepted way of life is fundamental. So is his faith in the ideals and principles which formed and continue to guide his work.

What are these and where to be found?

Through the years, Mr. Wright has written much and spoken often. Numerous books and periodicals (many among them rare or specialized), and private files as well, show his lively gift of narrative, his felicity at turning facts into lucid, inspiring examples of these very ideals and principles.

In order to make the principles and aims of Organic Architecture more generally available and understandable, the task remained to assemble statements dealing with architecture as Mr. Wright has experienced it and practiced it; to select strong, clear versions from several statements that recount one same event or explore one avenue of thought; and, by illustration, relate these to Mr. Wright's architecture. It is hoped this book accomplishes just that.

No claim of completeness can be made here in spite of Mr. Wright's generosity in making his files available, and the generosity of earlier editors and publishers whose works have been consulted. For the full story students must turn to the original documents and above all to the buildings themselves. Sources are credited and dates given, either of authorship or of first publication. The faults of this book are those of the editor alone, who is responsible for the present form of the texts and for the choice of illustrations.

The virtue of this book is Mr. Wright's; its graces are largely due to the help and guidance, here gratefully acknowledged, given by Mr. and Mrs. Wright and by the publisher and his staff.

E. K.

ARCHITECTURE   PRESENTS   MAN

PREFATORY

I hope the buildings shown on the following pages, and selected from among many as worthy, will serve again to illustrate basic principles which give to them all such vitality, integrity and magic as they have. I still hope to see these basic principles more comprehended, therefore the effects imitated less. No man's work need resemble mine. If he understands the working of the principles behind the effects he sees here, with similar integrity he will have his own way of building.

1951a

What a man does—*that* he has. You may find other things on him but they are not his.

1936a

Architects would do better and well enough were they to stick to their own last and do their own work quietly in their own way. I do not suppose that I myself have much right to be standing here preaching and talking to you of all this except as I have done this thing for a lifetime and swear never to try to tell you of something that I myself have not practiced and so do not really know.

1939a

"Except as I have done this thing for a lifetime"
Larkin Company administration building, Buffalo, N. Y., 1904

WHAT IS ARCHITECTURE?

What is architecture anyway? Is it the vast collection of the various buildings which have been built to please the varying taste of the various lords of mankind? I think not. No, I know that architecture is life; or at least it is life itself taking form and therefore it is the truest record of life as it was lived in the world yesterday, as it is lived today or ever will be lived. So architecture I know to be a Great Spirit. It can never be something which consists of the buildings which have been built by man on earth . . . mostly now rubbish heaps or soon to be. . . . Architecture is that great living creative spirit which from generation to generation, from age to age, proceeds, persists, creates, according to the nature of man, and his circumstances as they change. That is really architecture.

1939a

"Life itself taking form"
Zimmerman house, Manchester, Vt., 1953

In all buildings that man has built out of earth and upon the earth, his spirit, the pattern of him, rose great or small. It lived in his buildings. It still shows there. But common to all these workmanlike endeavors in buildings great or small, another spirit lived. Let us call this spirit, common to all buildings, the great spirit, architecture. Today we look back upon the endless succession of ruins that

are no more than the geological deposits washed into shore formation by the sea, landscape formed by the cosmic elements. These ancient buildings were similarly formed by the human spirit. It is the spirit elemental of architecture. The buildings are now dead to uses of present-day activity. They were sculptured by the spirit of architecture in passing, as inert shapes of the shore were sculptured by cosmic forces. Any building is a by-product of eternal living force, a spiritual force taking forms in time and place appropriate to man. They constitute a record to be interpreted, no letter to be imitated.

We carelessly call these ancient aggregations, architecture. Looking back upon this enormous deposit to man's credit, and keeping in mind that just as man was in his own time and place so was his building in its time and place, we must remember that architecture is not these buildings in themselves but far greater. We must believe architecture to be the living spirit that made buildings what they were. It is a spirit by and for man, a spirit of time and place. And we must perceive architecture, if we are to understand it at all, to be a spirit of the spirit of man that will live as long as man lives. It begins always at the beginning. It continues to bestrew the years with forms destined to change and to be strange to men yet to come.

"Taking form in time and place appropriate to man"
Project for Doheny ranch, California, 1921

19

We are viewing this valid record of the inspired work of the red men, yellow men, black men or white men of the human race in perspective outline. What we see is a vast human expression having a common ground of origin. It is more a part of man himself than the turtle's shell is part of the turtle. A great mass of matter has been eroded by man's spirit. These buildings were wrested by his tireless energy from the earth and erected in the eye of the sun. It was originally the conscious creation, out of man himself, of a higher self. His building, in order to be architecture, was the true spirit of himself made manifest (objective) whereas the turtle had no freedom of choice or any spirit at all in the making of his shell.

Considering this, we may now see wherein architecture is to be distinguished from mere building. Mere building may not know spirit at all. And it is well to say that the spirit of the thing is the essential life of that thing because it is truth. Such, in the retrospect, is the only life of architecture.   1937a

The center of architecture remains unchanged because—though all unconfessed or ill concealed—beauty is no less the true purpose of rational modern architectural endeavor than ever, just as beauty remains the essential characteristic of archi-

Coonley house, Riverside, Ill., 1908

V. C. Morris shop, San Francisco, Cal., 1947

21

Willey house, Minneapolis, Minn., 1934

tecture itself. But today because of scientific attainment the modern more clearly perceives beauty as integral order; order divined as an image by human sensibility; order apprehended by reason, executed by science. Yes, by means of a greater science, a more integral order may now be executed than any existing. With integral order once established you may perceive the rhythm of consequent harmony. To be harmonious is to be beautiful in a rudimentary sense: a good platform from which to spring toward the moving infinity that is the present. It is in architecture in this sense that "God meets with nature in the sphere of the relative." Therefore the first great necessity of a modern architecture is this keen sense of order as integral. That is to say the *form* itself in orderly relationship with purpose or function: the *parts* themselves in order with the form: the materials and methods of work in order with both: a kind of natural integrity—the integrity of each in all and of all in each. This is the exciting new order.

1931c

ORGANIC STRUCTURE IN NATURE

Primarily, nature furnished the materials for architectural motifs out of which the architectural forms as we know them today have been developed, and, although our practice for centuries has been for the most part to turn from her, seeking inspiration in books and adhering slavishly to dead formulae, her wealth of suggestion is inexhaustible; her riches greater than any man's desire. I know with what suspicion the man is regarded who refers matters of fine art back to nature. I know that it is usually an ill-advised return that is attempted, nature in external, obvious aspect is the usual sense of the term and the nature that is reached. But given inherent vision there is no source so fertile, so suggestive, so helpful aesthetically for the architect as a comprehension of natural law. As nature is never right for a picture so is she never right for the architect; that is, not ready-made. Nevertheless, she has beneath her more obvious forms a practical school in which a sense of proportion may be cultivated, when Vignola and Vitruvius fail as they must always fail. It is there that he may develop that sense of reality that translated to his own field in terms of his own work will lift him far above the realistic in his art; there the architect will be inspired by sentiment that will never degenerate to sentimentality and he will learn to draw with a surer hand the ever-perplexing and difficult line between the curious and the beautiful.

A sense of the organic is indispensable to an architect; where can he develop it so surely as in this school? A knowledge of the relations of form and function lies at the root of his practice; where else can he find the pertinent object lessons nature so readily furnishes? Where can he study the differentiations of form that go to determine character as he can study them in the trees? Where can that sense of inevitableness characteristic of a work of art be quickened as it may be by intercourse with nature in this sense?

1908a

No really Italian building seems ill at ease in Italy. All are happily content with what ornament and color they carry naturally. The native rocks and trees and garden slopes are at one with them. Wherever the cypress rises, there, like the touch of a magician's hand, all resolves into composition harmonious and complete.

The secret of this ineffable charm would be sought in vain in the rarefied air of scholasticism or in the ateliers of any pedantic fine art. It all lies closer to earth. Like a handful of moist, sweet earth itself. So simple that to modern minds trained in the intellectual gymnastics of "cultivated" taste it would seem unrelated to important purposes. So close to the heart it is that almost universally it is overlooked especially by the scholar.

As we pass along the wayside some blossom with unusually glowing color or prettiness of form attracts us. Held by it we gratefully accept its perfect loveliness. But, seeking the secret of its ineffable charm, we find the blossom whose more obvious claim first arrested our attention as nature intended, intimately related to the texture and shape of the foliage beneath it. We discover peculiar sympathy between the form of this flower and the system upon which leaves are arranged about the stalk. From this we are led on to observe a characteristic habit of growth and discover a resultant pattern of structure having first direction toward form deep down in roots hidden in the warm earth, kept moist there by a conservative covering of leaf-mould. *Structure*—as now we may observe—proceeds from generals to particulars arriving at the blossom, to attract us, proclaiming in its lines and form the nature of the structure that bore it. We have here a thing *organic*. Law and order are the basis of a finished grace and beauty. Beauty is the

expression of fundamental conditions in line, form and color true to those conditions and seeming to exist to fulfill them according to some thoughtful original design.

Though our intelligence may in no wise prove beauty the result of these harmonious internal conditions, that which through the ages appeals to our instinct as beautiful, we may realize, does not ignore these basic elements of law and order. Nor does it take long to establish in our minds the fact that no lasting beauty ever does ignore them. They are ever-present elements or are the actual conditions of the existence of beauty. From the study of the forms, or styles, which mankind has considered beautiful we see those living longest do in greatest measure fulfill these basic conditions. That anything grows is no concern of ours because the quality we call life, itself is beyond us. We are not necessarily concerned with that initial gift of life; and beauty, its essence, is for us as mysterious as life. All attempts to say what life is are foolish, like cutting out the head of our drum to find whence comes the sound. But we may study with profit these manifest truths of form and structure; facts of form as related to function; material traits of line determining character. We may deduce laws of procedure inherent in all natural growths, to use as basic principle for good building. We are ourselves a product of such natural law. These manifestations of principle are harmonious with the essence of our own being and so perceived by us to be good. We feel the good, true and beautiful to be essentially one with our own souls in any last analysis. Within us all there is at work a divine principle of growth to some good end. Accordingly we select as good whatever is in harmony with innate law.

We thus reach for the light, spiritually in some innate spirit-pattern as the plant does physically. If we are sound of heart and not sophisticated by our education far beyond our capacity, we call that objective the beautiful.

In other words, if and when we perceive anything to be beautiful we do instinctively recognize the rightness of that thing. This means that a glimpse of something essentially of the fiber of our own inner nature is revealed to us. Through his own deeper insight the artist shares with us this revelation. His power to visualize his conceptions or visions being greater than our own, a flash of truth from him stimulates us. We have a vision of innate harmony not fully understood today, though perhaps to be so appreciated tomorrow.

So we may say that knowledge of cause and effect in terms of line, color and form as found in organic nature will furnish us with certain guide lines along which any artist may sift materials, test motives and direct aims, thus roughly establishing at least a rational basis for nourishing his ideas and ideals of work.

Great artists usually do this by instinct. The thing *felt* is divined by inspiration perhaps, as synthetic analysis of their works will show. Poetry (it is always prophecy) is—in itself—no matter to be thus demonstrated. But what is of great value to every artist in his research is knowledge of those facts of relation; those inherent *qualities* of line, form and color which are in themselves a language of truth as well as of sentiment. . . .

1910a

Organic simplicity might everywhere be seen producing significant character in the ruthless but harmonious order I was taught to call nature. I was more than

familiar with it on the farm. All around me, I, or anyone for that matter, might see beauty in growing things and, by a little painstaking, learn how they grew to be beautiful. None was ever insignificant.

Mr. Wright's family farmland as he has landscaped it

1936a

"True *form* is always organic in character. It is really nature-pattern"

Only by patient study, to acquire knowledge of nature *in this interior sense,* are guiding principles ever to be established by the architect. Ideals gained by comprehension of these *organic* limitations are never lost. An artist having these may then defy his education. If he is really for nature in this inward sense he may be a rebel against his time and its laws but never lawless in his work nor as himself. 1910a

Meantime among so many disheartening discoveries stands the all-heartening important truth (something at least to tie to) that true FORM is always organic in character. It is really nature-pattern. In nature-abstraction, therefore, lies the difficulty as well as the simple center-line of the honest ego's search for integral FORM. . . . All form is a matter of structure. . . .

Proved by my own experience, I too can say that "every problem carries within itself its own solution," a solution to be reached only by the intense inner concentration of a sincere devotion to truth. I can say this out of a lively personal adventure in realizations that gives true scheme, line and color to all life and, so far as architecture goes, life to what otherwise would remain mere unrelated fact. Dust, even if stardust. 1943a

CREATIVITY

In the logic of the plan what we call standardization is seen to be fundamental groundwork in architecture. All things in nature exhibit this tendency to crystallize; to form mathematically and then to conform, as we may easily see. There is the fluid, elastic period of becoming, as in the plan, when possibilities are infinite.

"There is the fluid, elastic period of becoming, as in the plan, when possibilities are infinite" Sketch, plan for Ullman house, Oak Park, Ill., 1904

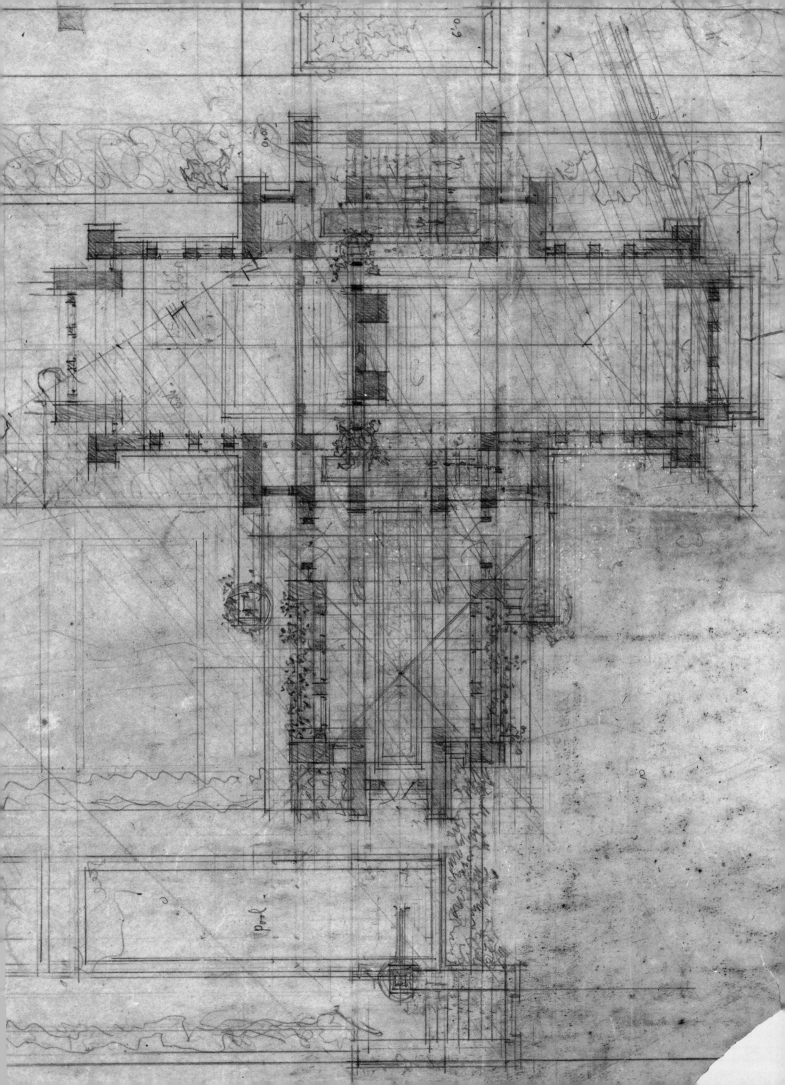

New effects may then originate from the idea or principle that conceives. Once form is achieved, however, that possibility is dead so far as it is a positive creative flux.

1928b

. . . Conceive the buildings in imagination, not first on paper but in the mind, thoroughly, before touching paper. Let the building, living in imagination, develop

Sketch perspective of Cheney house, Oak Park, Ill., 1904

gradually, taking more and more definite form before committing it to the drafting board. When the thing sufficiently lives for you then start to plan it with instruments, not before. To draw during the conception or sketch, as we say, experimenting with practical adjustments to scale, is well enough if the concept is clear enough to be firmly held meantime. But it is best always thus to cultivate the imagination from within. Construct and complete the building so far as you can before going to work on it with T square and triangle. Working with triangle and T square should be only to modify or extend or intensify or test the conception; finally to correlate the parts in detail.

If original concept is lost as the drawing proceeds, throw away all and begin afresh. To throw away a concept entirely to make way for a fresh one, that is a faculty of the mind not easily cultivated. Few architects have that capacity. It is perhaps a gift, but may be attained by practice. What I am trying to express is the fact that the plan is the gist of all truly creative matter and must gradually mature as such.

1928a

First came the general philosophy of the thing. . . . All artistic creation has its own philosophy. It is the first condition of creation. However, some would smile and say, the result of it.

Second, there was the general purpose of the whole to consider in each part: a matter of reasoned arrangement. This arrangement must be made with a sense of the yet-unborn whole in the mind, to be blocked out as appropriate to concrete masses cast in wooden boxes. Holding all this diversity together in a preconceived direction is really no light matter but is the condition of creation. Imagination conceives here the PLAN suitable to the material and the purpose of the whole, seeing the probably possible form clearer all the time.

Imagination reigns supreme, until now the form the whole will naturally take must be seen.

But if all this preliminary planning has been well conceived that question in the main is settled. This matter of style is organic now.

We do not choose the style. No. Style is what is coming now and it will be what we are in all this. A thrilling moment in any architect's experience. He is about to see the countenance of something he is invoking with intense concentration. Out of this inner sense of order and love of the beauty of life something is to be born—maybe to live long as a message of hope and be a joy or a curse to his kind. His message he feels. None the less will it be "theirs," and rather more. And it is out of love and understanding that any building is born to bless 1932a   or curse those it is built to serve. . . .

An aid to creative effort, the open fire. What a friend to the laboring artist the poetic baked-onion! Real encouragement to him is great music. Yes, and what a poor creature, after all, creation comes singing through. About like catgut and horsehair in the hands of a Sarasate.

Night labor at the drafting board is best for intense creation. It may continue uninterrupted.

Meantime glancing side reflections are passing in the mind—"design is abstraction of nature-elements in purely geometric terms"—that is what we ought to call pure design? . . . This cube—this square—proportion. But—nature-pattern and nature-texture in materials themselves often approach conventionalization, or the abstract, to such a degree as to be superlative means ready to the designer's hand to qualify, stimulate, and enrich his own efforts. . . . What texture this concrete

"This cube—this square—proportion"
Unity Church, Oak Park, Ill., 1906

mass? Why not its own gravel? How to bring the gravel clean on the surface? . . . I knew. Here was reality. Yes, the "fine thing" is always reality. Always reality? . . . Realism, the subgeometric, however, is the abuse of this fine feeling. . . . Keep the straight lines clean and keep all significant of the idea—the flat plane expressive and always clean cut. But let texture come into them to qualify them in sunlight.

Reality is spirit—the essence brooding just behind all aspect. Seize it! And—after all you will see that the pattern of reality is supergeometric, casting a spell or a charm over any geometry, and is such a spell in itself.

Yes, so it seems to me as I draw with T square, triangle and scale. That is what it means to be an artist—to seize this essence brooding everywhere in everything, just behind aspect. These questionings arising each with its own train of thought by the way, as the architect sits at his work.

1932a   Suddenly it is morning. To bed for a while.

Of course what is most vitally important in all that I have tried to say and explain cannot be explained at all. It need not be, I think. But here in this searching process may be seen the architect's mind at work, as boys in the studio would crowd around and participate in it. And you too, perhaps, may see certain wheels go around.

Certain hints coming through between the lines that may help someone who 1932a   needs help in comprehending what planning a building really means.

To idealize in the fanciful sketch is a thing unknown to me. Except as I were given some well-defined limitations or requirements—the more specific the better —there would be no problem, nothing to work with, nothing to work out; why 1931b   then trouble . . . ?

The most pleasurable thing I could imagine was that I might go into some shop where fine colored pencils were kept and gather several of every color I had ever seen and perhaps see some never seen before. Perhaps a more gorgeous red, a truer blue, a warmer green. And I would lay them all out in a row, abuse the white paper on the board at which I sat; and sit looking at them, several of each and every possible color. Enough to use and last some time, for once. . . . But I love colored pencils. They are intimately associated with my sense of happiness, and 1932e   have been since childhood.

Don't you know that all artistic expression is in the nature of inner experience? It is not something up here in the head at all. It's something in here, the heart. Coupled with this, the head, this is awareness of what's going on, but without this, the heart, even the head can't help you.

You must know that creative work is not the province of the amateur. Except as you can put a capital A on that word amateur and consider the Amateur as the lover, loving something deeply enough and strongly enough to sacrifice even his *life* for it. Until then, you won't find yourself in it.

1953b

THE PLACE OF THE MACHINE IN ARCHITECTURE

Consider well that a house is a machine in which to live but architecture begins where that concept of the house ends. All life is machinery in a rudimentary sense, and yet machinery is the life of nothing. Machinery is machinery only because of life. It is better to proceed from the generals to the particulars; so do not rationalize from machinery to life, why not think from life to machines? The utensil, the weapon, the automaton—all are *appliances*. The song, the masterpiece, the edifice are a warm outpouring of the heart of man—human delight in life triumphant: we glimpse the infinite.

That glimpse or vision is what makes art a matter of inner experience—therefore sacred, and no less but rather more individual in this age, I assure you, than ever before.

Architecture expresses human life, machines do not, nor does any appliance whatsoever. Appliances only serve life.

1931c

We need the engineering architect. Profession or no profession. An architect not only familiar with shopwork and factory conditions in America but an architect who can sense the human benefits actually to be derived from mechanized production that might make our living in a machine age less destructive to individuality, not more and more destructive. The engineer can no more accomplish this than a professor of mathematics can make music.

1930b

Why should architecture or objects of art in the machine age, just because they are made by machines, have to resemble machinery? Because they were so made might be the best of reasons why they should not. Nor is there good reason why forms stripped clean of all considerations but function and utility should be admirable beyond that standpoint. They may be abominable from the human standpoint. Let us have no fear, therefore, of liberalism in our art of architecture nor in our industries. . . .

1930a

The machine can be nowhere creator except as it may be a good tool in the creative artist's tool box. It is only when you try to make a living thing of the machine itself that you begin to betray your human birthright. The machine can do great work—yes—but only when well in hand of one who does not overestimate its resources, one who knows how to put it to suitable work for the human being.

S. C. Johnson and Son general offices, Racine, Wis., 1936

The proper use of the machine should be to make life more beautiful, more livable. No, not necessarily easier and quicker just to feed this American voracity which we call speed. If speed and destruction plus sanitation are to be the function of machinery among us, the machine will destroy us and its present idolatry will eventually defeat our attempt at a culture.

1951a

Already, when I began to build, commercial machine standardization had taken

Typical 1880's house,
Oak Park Ill.,

the life of handicraft. Outworn handicraft had never troubled me, but to make new forms, living expressions of the new order of the machine, and to continue what was noble in tradition did trouble me. I wanted to realize genuine new forms true to the spirit of great tradition and found I should have to make them; appropriate to the old (natural) and to new (synthetic) materials; but furthermore I should have to design them so that the machine (or process) that must make them could and would make them better than anything could possibly be made by hand.

1936a

The character and brutal power as well as the opportunity for beauty of our own age were coming clear to me. In fact I saw then as now that they are all one. I saw our own great chance in this sense still going to waste on every side. Rebel-

Office court, Larkin Company
building, Buffalo, N. Y., 1904

lious and protestant as I was myself when the Larkin Building came from me, I
was conscious also that the only way to succeed, either as rebel or as protestant,
was to make architecture genuine and constructive affirmation of the new order
1932a of this machine age.

These buildings, this architecture I myself have created, is simply a lifelong,
fully conscious, unremitting effort to render the machine—this tool of modern
times—so useful that a great indigenous culture we could honestly call American
might occur. A living expression of the greatness of the human spirit of our nation
might be ours. So what quality you perceive in these buildings must be the reflection

of a truly religious endeavor to make beauty of environment come alive again for our own peoples; to make them aware of the richness of a life they now almost wholly miss. This innate richness of life can be theirs only when they learn how to command, restrain and use the machine properly, that is to say as a mere tool instead of falling into the worship of it as a moneymaker.

1951a

I have . . . seemed to belittle the nature of our time and the great achievements of science, but I have intended to do neither because I believe human nature still sound and recognize that science has done a grand job well; but well I know that science cannot save us. Science can give us only the tools in the box, mechanical miracles that it has already given us. But of what use to us are miraculous tools until we have mastered the humane, cultural use of them? We do not want to live in a world where the machine has mastered the man; we want to live in a world where man has mastered the machine!

1939a

ARCHITECTURE IS POETRY

No rationalizing of the machine nor factorializing of aesthetics can obscure the fact that architecture is born, not made—must consistently grow from within to whatever it becomes. Such forms as it takes must be spontaneous generation of materials, building methods and purpose. The brain is a great tool with great craft; but in architecture you are concerned with our sense of the specific beauty of human lives as lived on earth in relation to each other. Organic architecture seeks a superior sense of use and a finer sense of comfort, expressed in organic simplicity. That is what you, young man, should call *architecture*. Use and comfort in order to become architecture must become *spiritual satisfactions* wherein the soul insures a more subtle use, achieves a more constant repose. So, architecture speaks as poetry to the soul.

1931c

A good building is the greatest of poems when it is organic architecture. The building faces and is reality and serves while it releases life; daily life is better worth living and all the necessities are happier because of useful living in a building none the less poetry, but more truly so. Every great architect is—necessarily—a great poet.

1939a

Heurtley house, Oak Park, Ill., 1902

Detail, Taliesin, Spring Green, Wis., 1925

TRUST IN LIFE

Sketch for Oak Park (Ill.)
Playground Association, 1926

I have learned in my lifetime that there is only one trust worthy of any man and that is trust in life itself; the firm belief that life *is* (worlds without end, amen) that you cannot cheat it nor can you defeat it.

We *know* that life is to be trusted. We *know* that the *interpretation* of life is the true function of the architect because we know that buildings are made for life, to be lived in and to be lived in happily, designed to contribute to that living, joy and living beauty.

1939a

THE IMPORTANCE OF FOLK BUILDING

... The true basis for any serious study of the art of Architecture still lies in those indigenous, more humble buildings everywhere that are to architecture what folklore is to literature or folk song to music and with which academic architects were seldom concerned. In the aggregate of these simple buildings lie traits which make them characteristically Italian, French, Dutch, German, Spanish, or English as the case may be. These many folk structures are *of the soil,* natural. Though often slight, their virtue is intimately related to environment and to the heart-life of the people. Functions are usually truthfully conceived and rendered invariably with natural feeling. Results are often beautiful and always instructive.

1910a

APHORISMS ON ARCHITECTURE

So modern architecture rejects the major axis and the minor axis of classic architecture. It rejects all grandomania, every building that would stand in military fashion heels together, eyes front, something on the right hand and something on the left hand. Architecture already favors the reflex, the natural easy attitude, the

View from kitchen toward drafting room, Taliesin West, Scottsdale, Ariz., 1938

occult symmetry of grace and rhythm affirming the ease, grace, and naturalness of natural life. Modern architecture—let us now say *organic* architecture—is a natural architecture—the architecture of nature, for nature.

1939a

First, a study of the nature of materials you elect to use and the tools you must use with them, searching to find the characteristic qualities in both that are suited to your purpose. Second, with an ideal of organic nature as a guide, so to unite these qualities to serve that purpose, that the fashion of what you do has integrity or is natively fit, regardless of preconceived notions of style. Style is a by-product of the process and comes of the man or the mind in the process. The style of the thing, therefore, will be the man; it is his. Let his forms alone.

1914a

...Look with scorn and suspicion upon all efforts to create the beautiful without an underlying sense and knowledge of what constitutes good building, good structure.

1953b

... When we endeavor to make for ourselves an *atmosphere* in which to live and work according to our own faith and feeling for nature, we are performing 1953b   a genuine service not only to our time, but especially to the future....

... Buildings perform their highest function in relation to human life within and the natural efflorescence without; and to develop and maintain the harmony of a true chord between them, making of the building in this sense a sure foil for 1908a   life, broad simple surfaces and highly conventionalized forms are inevitable....

Unity Church, Oak Park, Ill., 1906

There should be as many types of house as there are types of people, and as many differentiations of the types as there are different people. 1896a

Architecture is the scientific art of making structure express ideas. 1930a

Architecture is the triumph of human imagination over materials, methods and men, to put man into possession of his own earth. 1930a

Architecture is man's great sense of himself embodied in a world of his own making. It may rise as high in quality only as its source because great art is great life. 1930a

First . . . is the nature of materials; second, is that characteristic architectural element, the third dimension; and third, there is integral ornament. This neglected trinity, it seems to me, constitutes the beating heart of the whole matter of architecture so far as art is concerned.

Surface and mass, relatively superficial, however machine-made or however much resembling machinery, are . . . by-products, or will be when architecture arises out of the matter. If proof is needed we shall find it as we go along together. . . . 1931b

Machinery, materials and men—yes—these are the stuffs by means of which the so-called American architect will get his architecture, if there is any such architect and America ever gets any architecture of her own. Only by the strength of his spirit's grasp upon all three—machinery, materials and men—will the architect be able so to build that his work may be worthy the great name architecture. 1931b

A great architecture is greatest proof of human greatness. 1931b

THE LAW OF CHANGE

Let our universities realize and teach that *the law of organic change is the only thing that mankind can know as beneficent or as actual!* We can only know that all things are in process of flowing in some continuous state of becoming. Heraclitus was stoned in the streets of Athens for a fool for making that declaration of independence, I do not remember how many hundreds of years ago.

1939a

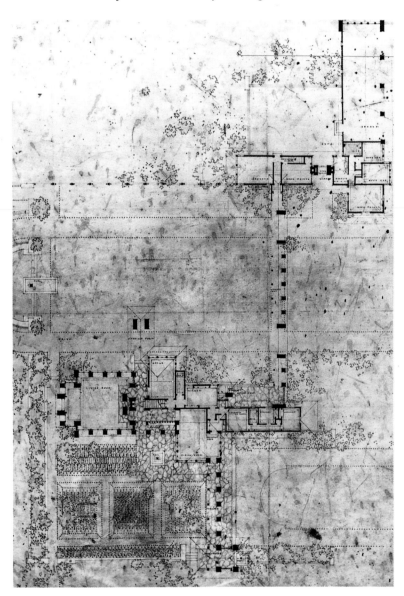

Plan for Cutten house, Downer's Grove, Ill., 1911

FROM GENERALS TO PARTICULARS

PRELIMINARY

Repose is the highest quality in the art of architecture, next to integrity, and a
1931b   reward for integrity.

Do not imagine that repose means taking it easy for the sake of a rest, but
rather taking it easily because perfectly adjusted in relation to the whole, in
absolute poise, leaving nothing but a feeling of quiet satisfaction with its sense
1894a   of completeness.

Walter house, Quasqueton,
Iowa, 1949

Architecture, to us at Taliesin, is the great mother art. We feel and see architecture not only as the basic structure of what we call our environment, now so
uncultured, but also its integrity. Only our own creative ability can give us beauty
as native evidence of ourselves: a quality of peace. We mean this quality when we
1951a   use the word repose.

INTEGRITY

One day in 1908 Mrs. Avery Coonley, an aristocratic leader in Chicago,
appeared at the Oak Park studio and asked me to do a house for her and her
husband in Riverside. They had been around to see everything I had done—
not so difficult then—and she said, "Mr. Wright, we have come to you, because
of all the buildings we have seen, yours seem to wear the countenance of principle."
1953a   Naturally, after that they had the very best I was capable of.

Preliminary design, Coonley house, Riverside, Ill., 1908

... With this ideal of internal order as integral in architecture supreme in my mind, I would have done nothing less even could I have commanded armies of craftsmen. By now had come the discipline of a great ideal. There is no discipline, architectural or otherwise, so severe, but there is no discipline that yields such rich rewards in work nor is there any discipline so safe and sure of results as this ideal of internal order, the integration that is organic. Lesser ideas took flight, like birds, from this exacting, informing ideal, always in the same direction, but further on each occasion for flight until great goals were in sight. 1931c

I have endeavored ... to establish a harmonious relationship between ground plan and elevation of these buildings, considering the one as a solution and the other an expression of the conditions of a problem of which the whole is a project. I have tried to establish an organic integrity to begin with, forming the basis for the subsequent working out of a significant grammatical expression and making the whole, as nearly as I could, consistent. 1908a

You see, by way of concentrated thought, the idea is likely to spring into life all at once and be completed eventually with the unity of a living organism. In architecture each new plan will have its own grammar and law of growth. An inner module of space measured by a unit system in plan as well as elevation makes

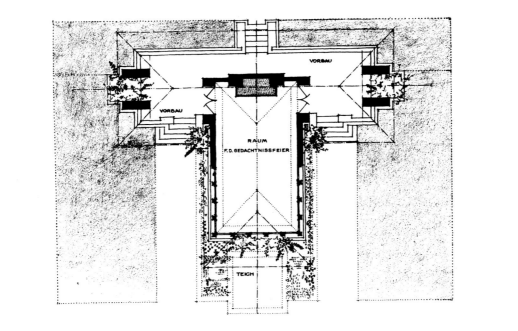

"A harmonious relationship between ground plan and elevation—one as a solution and the other an expression"
Plan and perspective, Pettit memorial chapel, Belvidere, Ill.

Project for cabin amid big trees, part of a development for Lake Tahoe, Cal., 1922

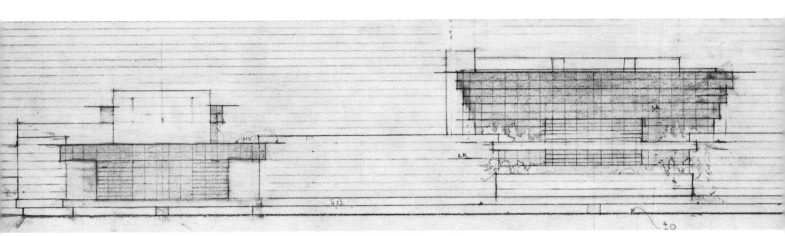

each detail proportionate in any plan we make, each part an inevitable and well-proportioned portion of the whole. Thus we arrive at entity and atmosphere. Only entity lives.

... There is no possible transfer of the same grammar from one genuine building to the other. The law of growth for the Johnson ... laboratory is as different from that of Taliesin West, say, as the oak tree from the cactus. But both are alike in having an inner concept and consistency of grammar. Each is true to itself.

1951a

"A unit system in plan as well as elevation"
Sketch for House on the Mesa, 1931

"There is no possible transfer of the same grammar from one genuine building to the other"
Left: hallway near kitchen, Taliesin West, Scottsdale, Ariz., 1938; right: bridge over driveway, S. C. Johnson and Son office building, Racine, Wis., 1936

ONE THING INSTEAD OF MANY THINGS

The differentiation of a single, certain, simple form characterizes the expression of one building. Quite a different form may serve for another, but from one basic idea all the formal elements of design are in each case derived and held well together in scale and character. The form chosen may flare outward, opening flowerlike to the sky; another, droop to accentuate artistically the weight of the masses; another be noncommittal or abruptly emphatic, or its grammar may be deduced from some plant form that has appealed to me, as certain properties in line and form of the sumac were used in the Lawrence house at Springfield; but

"To let individual elements arise and shine at the expense of final repose is . . . a betrayal of trust"
Hollyhock House, Hollywood, Cal. 1917

in every case the motif is adhered to throughout so that it is not too much to say that each building aesthetically is cut from one piece of goods and consistently hangs together with an integrity impossible otherwise.

The method in itself does not of necessity produce a beautiful building, but it does provide a framework as a basis which has an organic integrity, susceptible to the architect's imagination and at once opening to him nature's wealth of artistic suggestion, ensuring him a guiding principle within which he can never be wholly false, out of tune, or lacking in rational motif. The subtleties, the shifting blending harmonies, the cadences, the nuances, are a matter of his own nature, his own susceptibilities and faculties.

But self-denial is imposed upon the architect to a far greater extent than upon any other artist-creator. The temptation to sweeten work, to make each detail in itself lovable and expressive, is always great; but that the whole may be truly eloquent of its ultimate function, restraint is imperative. To let individual elements arise and shine at the expense of final repose is for the architect a betrayal of trust, for buildings are the background or framework for the human life within their walls and a foil for the nature efflorescent without. So architecture is the most complete of conventionalizations and of all the arts the most subjective except music.

In most of the interiors there will be found a quiet, a simple dignity that we imagine is only to be found in the old and it is due to the underlying organic harmony, to the each in all and the all in each throughout. This is the modern oppor-

Pauson house, Phoenix, Ariz., 1940

tunity, to make of a building, together with its equipment, appurtenances and environment, an entity which shall constitute a complete work of art; and a work of art more valuable to society as a whole than has before existed because discordant conditions, endured for centuries, are smoothed away; everyday life here finds an expression germane to its daily existence; an idealization of the common need, sure to be uplifting and helpful in the same sense that pure air to breathe is better than air poisoned with noxious gases.

1908a

I have tried to make their grammar perfect in its way and to give their forms and proportions an integrity that will bear study, although few of them can be intelligently studied apart from their environment. So, what might be termed the democratic character of the exteriors is their first undefined offense: the lack,

Tomek house, Riverside, Ill., 1907

wholly, of what the professional critic would deem architecture; in fact, most of the critic's architecture has been left out.

As for the future, the work shall grow more truly simple; more expressive with fewer lines; fewer forms; more articulate with less labor; more plastic; more fluent, although more coherent; more organic. It shall grow . . . to fit more perfectly the methods and processes that are called upon to produce it. . . .

1908a

Thus to make of a human dwelling place a complete work of art, in itself expressive and beautiful, intimately related to modern life and fit to live in, lending itself freely and suitably to the individual needs of the dwellers so far as itself is an harmonious entity, fitting in color, pattern and nature the requirements of utility and really an expression of them in character—this is the tall modern American opportunity in architecture. True basis for a true culture. Once founded, this will become a new tradition: a vast step in advance of the prescribed fashion when a dwelling was a composite of separate rooms: chambers to contain mere aggregations of furniture, lacking utility and comforts. An organic entity, this modern building, as contrasted with that former insensate aggregation of parts. Surely we have here the higher ideal of *unity* as a more intimate working out of the expression of one's life in one's environment. One thing instead of many things; a great thing instead of a collection of small ones.

1910a

Rosenbaum house, Florence, Ala., 1939

In organic architecture then, it is quite impossible to consider the building as one thing, its furnishings another and its setting and evironment still another. The spirit in which these buildings are conceived sees all these together at work *as one thing*. All are to be studiously foreseen and provided for in the nature of the structure. All these should become mere details of the character and completeness of the structure. Incorporated . . . are lighting, heating and ventilation. The very chairs and tables, cabinets and even musical instruments, where practicable, are *of* the building itself, never fixtures upon it. No appliances or fixtures are to be admitted where circumstances permit the full development of the organic character of the building-scheme.

Floor coverings and hangings are at least as much a part of the house as the plaster on the walls or the tiles on the roof. This feature called furnishings has given most trouble so far and is least satisfactory to myself. . . . To make necessary appurtenances into elements of architecture themselves sufficiently light, graceful and flexible . . . requires much more time and thought on my part as well as more money to spend, than is usually forthcoming in our country at this time. But in time this may be accomplished by improvements in all stock articles, still comparatively primitive. Yet stoves and radiators have disappeared, lighting fixtures are becoming incorporated, floor coverings and hangings are becoming textured instead of patterned and many stock things even now are easily adapted to conform. Chairs as informal movable articles of common use are still unsolved in most cases. Although I have designed them in feeling with the building I am not satisfied with the comfort they provide.

1910a

Soon I found it difficult, anyway, to make some of the furniture in the abstract. That is, to design it as architecture and make it human at the same time—fit for human use. I have been black and blue in some spot, somewhere, almost all my life from too intimate contact with my own early furniture.

Dining area, Lewis house,
Libertyville, Ill., 1940

56

"Impossible to consider the building as one thing, its furnishings another"
Living room, Lewis house, Libertyville, Ill., 1940

Human use and comfort should not be taxed to pay for any designer's idiosyncrasy. Human use and comfort should have intimate possession of every interior—

An early photo of Taliesin loggia, Spring Green, Wis., 1925

A recent photo of Taliesin loggia, Spring Green, Wis., 1925

should be felt in every exterior. Decoration is intended to make use more charming
1932a and comfort more appropriate, or else a privilege has been abused.

However, there are no decorations nor is there any place for them in this architecture. The easel picture, for instance, has no place on the walls. It is regarded as
music might be, suited to a mood and provided for in a recess of the wall if desired,
where a door might be dropped like the cover of a portfolio and the particular
thing desired, revealed and studied for a time; left exposed for several days perhaps, to give place to another; or, entirely put away by simply closing the wooden
portfolio. Easel pictures might then be possible. Great pictures, on the other hand,
should have their gallery; oratorio is not performed in a drawing room. The piano
or organ wherever possible may and should disappear into the structure, the key-
board or whatever openwork or tracery is necessary for sound to emerge, the
only visible feature. Dining table and chairs are easily managed with the architec-
1910a ture of the building. Only so far as this has development progressed.

In the Midway Gardens built in Chicago in 1913 I tried to complete the synthesis: planting, furnishings, music, painting, and sculpture, all to be one. But I found musicians, painters, and sculptors were unable to rise at that time to any such synthesis. Only in a grudging and dim way did most of them even understand it as an idea. So I made the designs for all to harmonize with the architecture; crude as any sketch is crude, incomplete as to execution, but in effect sufficiently complete to show the immense importance of any such attempt on any architect's part and show, indeed, that only so does architecture completely live.   1936a

Exterior and interior ornament, Midway Gardens,
Chicago, Ill., 1914

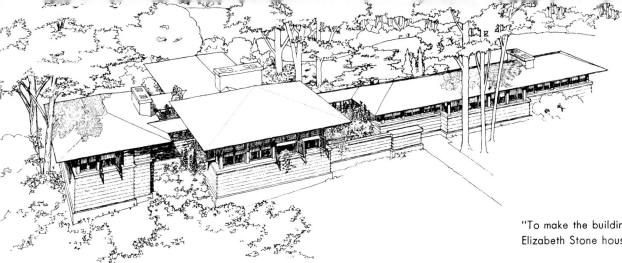

EARTH-LINE AND HUMAN SCALE—THE SENSE OF SHELTER

I see this extended horizontal line as the true earth-line of human life, indicative of freedom. Always.

1943a

The broad expanded plane is the horizontal plane infinitely extended. In that lies such freedom for man on this earth as he may call his.

1943a

I had an idea (it still seems to be my own) that the planes parallel to the earth in buildings identify themselves with the ground, do most to make the buildings belong to the ground. (Unluckily they defy the photographer.) At any rate, independently I perceived this fact and put it to work. I had an idea that every house in that low region should begin *on* the ground, not *in* it as they then began, with damp cellars. This feeling became an idea also; eliminated the basement. I devised one at ground level. And the feeling that the house should *look* as though it began there *at* the ground put a projecting base course as a visible edge to this foundation where, as a platform, it was evident preparation for the building itself and welded the structure to the ground.

An idea (probably rooted deep in instinct) that *shelter* should be the essential look of any dwelling, put the low spreading roof, flat or hipped or low-gabled with generously projecting eaves, over the whole. I began to see a building primarily not as a cave but as broad shelter in the open, related to vista; vista without and vista within. You may see in these various feelings all taking the same direction that I was born an American, child of the ground and of space, welcoming spaciousness as a modern human need, as well as learning to see it as the natural human opportunity. The farm had no negligible share in developing this sense of things in me, I am sure.

1936a

At Taliesin, Spring Green, Wis., 1925

At Taliesin West, Scottsdale, Ariz. 1938

Before this, by way of innate sense of comfort, had come the idea that the size of the human figure should fix every proportion of a dwelling or of anything in it. Human scale was true building scale. Why not, then, the scale fixing the proportions of all buildings whatsoever? What other scale could I use? This was not a canon taught me by anyone. So I accommodated heights in the new buildings to no exaggerated established order nor to impress the beholder (I hated grandomania then as much as I hate it now) but only to comfort the human being. I knew the house dweller could seldom afford enough built-in or built-over space to move about in freely, perceiving the horizontal line as the earth-line of human life (the line of repose), this an individual sense of the thing began to bear fruit. I first extended horizontal spacing without enlarging the building by cutting out all the room partitions that did not serve the kitchen or give needed privacy for sleeping apartments or (as in the day of the parlor) serve to prevent some formal intrusion into the intimacy of the family circle. The small social office I set aside as a necessary evil to receive callers, for instance. Even this one concession soon disappeared. . . .

To get the house down to the horizontal in appropriate proportion and into quiet relationship with the ground and as a more humane consideration anyway, the servants had to come down out of the complicated attic and go into a separate unit of their own attached to the kitchen on the ground floor. They liked this compulsion, though the housewife worried. Closets disappeared as unsanitary boxes wasteful of room and airy wardrobes cut in the rooms served instead.

"Human scale was true building scale"
Sketch of cabin for Como Orchard Community, Darby, Mont, 1910

Freedom of floor space and elimination of useless heights worked a miracle in the new dwelling place. A sense of appropriate freedom had changed its whole

1936a

aspect. The dwelling became more fit for human habitation . . . and more natural to its site. An entirely new sense of space values in architecture began to come home. It now appears that it then first came into the architecture of the modern world. This was about 1893. Certainly something of the kind was due.

THE EARLY DAYS OF ORGANIC ARCHITECTURE

To reiterate the statement made in 1908: this ideal of an organic architecture for America was touched by Richardson and Root, and perhaps other men; but was developing consciously twenty-eight years ago in the practice of Adler and Sullivan when I went to work in their office. This ideal combination, Adler and Sullivan, was then working to produce what no other combination of architects nor any individual architect at that time dared even preach: a sentient, rational building that would owe its style to the integrity with which it was individually fashioned for its particular purpose; a thinking as well as a feeling process, requir-

1914a

ing the independent work of true artist imagination. . . .

The old architecture, always dead for me so far as its grammar went, began literally to disappear. As if by magic new effects came to life as though by them-

65

selves and I could draw inspiration from nature herself. I was beholden to no man for the look of anything. Textbook for me? "The book of creation." No need any more to be a wanderer among the objects and traditions of the past, picking and choosing his way by the idiosyncrasy of taste, guided only by personal predilection. From this hell I had been saved. The world lost an eclectic and gained an interpreter. If I did not like the Gods now I could make better ones.

1936a

Of course, I will never forget the sensations when the Winslow House was built in 1893 in Oak Park, Ill., the year I left Adler and Sullivan and started my own practice. All Oak Park and River Forest began prowling around the place.

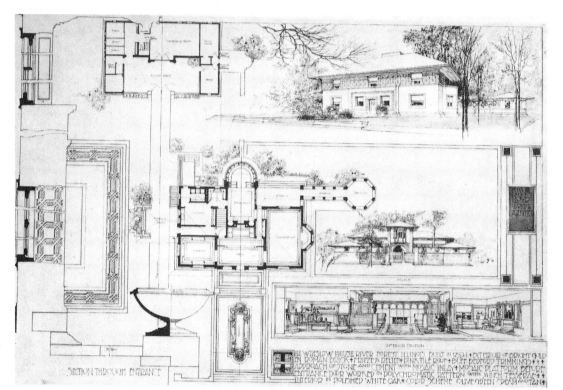

Winslow house, River Forest, Ill., 1893

I remember climbing up into an upper part of the building during construction to listen to comments. I pulled the ladder up and waited. In came a young fellow with a couple of young women and the fellow said, "Have you seen the man who built this? God, he looks as if he had a pain." Another one said, "They say this cost $30,000, but I can't see it." I learned my lesson: I never listened like that again.

With that house, in the realm of residence, modern architecture began to make its appearance in the United States, and that would mean in the world. I remember the feeling aroused in me of wonder at the amazement and astonishment that house had created. It was the talk of the town. One man said, "I've seen that house of Winslow's. I wouldn't want to build anything that made me take the back road to the station to avoid being laughed at." It was some time before my fortunes as a young architect recovered from those reactions.

1953a

The first thing to do was to get rid of the attic and, therefore, of the dormer and of the useless heights below it. And next, get rid of the unwholesome basement, entirely—yes, absolutely—in any house built on the prairie. Instead of lean brick chimneys, bristling up from steep roofs to hint at Judgment everywhere, I could see necessity for one only, a broad generous one, or at most for two, these kept low down on gently sloping roofs or perhaps flat roofs. The big fireplace below, inside, became now a place for a real fire, justified the great size of this chimney outside. A real fireplace at that time was extraordinary. There were then

Taliesin, Spring Green, Wis., 1925

mantels instead. A mantel was a marble frame for a few coals, or piece of wooden furniture with tiles stuck in it and a grate, the whole set slam up against the wall. The mantel was an insult to comfort, but the *integral* fireplace became an important part of the building itself in the houses I was allowed to build out there on the prairie. It refreshed me to see the fire burning deep in the masonry of the house itself.

Taking a human being for my scale, I brought the whole house down in height to fit a normal man; believing in no other scale, I broadened the mass out, all I possibly could, as I brought it down into spaciousness. It has been said that were I three inches taller (I am 5′ 8½″ tall), all my houses would have been quite different in proportion. Perhaps.

1931b

. . . It will be noticed that all the structures stand upon their foundations to the eye as well as physically. There is good, substantial preparation at the ground for

Detail, Martin house, Buffalo, N.Y., 1904

all the buildings and it is the first grammatical expression of all the types. This preparation, or water table, is to these buildings what the stylobate was to the ancient Greek temple. To gain it, it was necessary to reverse the established practice of setting the supports of the building to the outside of the wall, to set them to the inside so as to leave the necessary support for the outer base. This was natural enough and good enough construction but many an owner was disturbed by private information from the practical contractor to the effect that he would have his whole house in the cellar if he submitted to it. This was at the time a marked innovation, though the most natural thing in the world, and to me, to this day, indispensable.

With this innovation established, one of the odds and ends usual in walls, the horizontal stripe of the foundation above ground, was eliminated and . . . a simple, unbroken wall surface from foot to level of second story sill was secured. At that point a change of material occurred to form the simple frieze. . . . Even this was 1908a frequently omitted . . . the wall let alone from base to cornice or eaves.

Sometimes it was possible to make the enclosing wall from the second-story window sill clear down to the ground, a heavy wainscot of fine masonry materials resting on the cement or stone platform laid on the foundation. I liked that wainscot to be of masonry material when my clients felt they could afford it.

House walls were now to be started at the ground on a cement or stone water table that looked like a low platform under the building, which it usually was, but the house walls were stopped at the second story window-sill level, to let the rooms above come through in a continuous window series, under the broad eaves of a gently sloping overhanging roof. This made enclosing screens out of the lower walls as well as light screens out of the second story walls. Here was true *enclosure* 1931b *of interior space.* A new sense of building, it seems.

As the wall surfaces were simplified and emphasized, fenestration became exceedingly difficult and more than ever important. I used to gloat over the beautiful buildings I could build if only it were unnecessary to cut holes in them; but at first the holes were managed frankly as in the Winslow house and later as elementary constituents of the structure, grouped in rhythmical fashion, so that all the light and air and prospect the most rabid client could wish would not be too much from an artistic standpoint; of this achievement I am proud. The window groups are 1908a managed, too, whenever required, so that overhanging eaves do not shade them.

In this sense I was working away at the wall as a wall and bringing it towards the function of a screen, a means of opening up space which, as control of building materials improved, would finally permit the free use of the whole space without affecting the soundness of the structure.

The climate being what it was, violent in extremes of heat and cold, damp and dry, dark and bright, I gave broad protecting roof shelter to the whole, getting back to the purpose for which the cornice was originally designed. The underside of roof projections was flat and usually light in color to create a glow of reflected light that softly brightened the upper rooms. Overhangs had double value: shelter and preservation for the walls of the house, as well as this diffusion of reflected light for the upper story through the light screens now often windows in long series.

At this time, a house to me was obvious primarily as interior space under fine *shelter.* I liked the sense of shelter in the look of the building. I achieved it, I believe.

What I have just described was all on the *outside* of the house and was there chiefly because of what happened *inside.*

. . . I declared the whole lower floor one room, cutting off the kitchen as a laboratory, putting servants' sleeping and living quarters next to it, semidetached, on

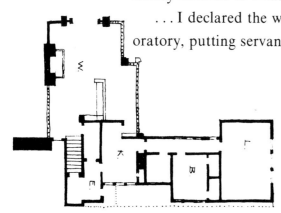

Project for Walter Gerts house,
Glencoe, Ill., 1902

70

the ground floor, screening various portions in the big room, for certain domestic purposes—like dining or reading, or receiving a formal caller. There were no plans like these in existence at the time but my clients were pushed towards these ideas as helpful to a solution of the vexed servant problem. Scores of unnecessary doors disappeared and no end of partition. Both clients and servants liked the new freedom. The house became more free as space and more livable too. Interior spaciousness began to dawn.

Having got window openings and doors lined up and lowered to convenient human height, the ceilings of the rooms, too, could be brought over on to the walls,

Dining room, Waller house, River Forest, Ill., 1899

by way of the horizontal, broad bands of plaster on the walls above the windows, the plaster colored the same as the room ceilings. This would bring the ceiling surface down to the very window tops. The ceilings thus expanded, by extending them downward as the wall band above the windows, gave a generous overhead to even small rooms. The sense of the whole was broadened and made plastic, too, by this means.

1931b

Here entered the important new element of plasticity—as I saw it, indispensable element to a successful use of the machine, to true modernity. The windows would

sometimes be wrapped around the building corners as inside emphasis of plasticity and to increase the sense of interior space. I fought for outswinging windows because the casement window associated house with the out-of-doors, gave free openings outward. In other words, the so-called casement was not only simple but more human in use and effect. So more natural. If it had not existed I should have invented it. But it was not used at that time in the United States.

I used double-hung windows once, in the Winslow house, and rejected them forever thereafter. Nor at that time did I entirely eliminate the wooden trim. I did make the trim light and continuously flowing, that is to say, gave it plasticity instead of accepting the prevailing heavy cut-and-butt carpenter work. As I laid it out, the machine could do it all perfectly well. There was need of that much trim then to conceal poor workmanship, because the battle between the machines and 1932a the union had already begun to demoralize workmen. Clients would come ready to accept any innovation but "those swinging windows," and when in the nature of the proposition they must take them or leave the rest, they frequently employed "the other fellow" to give them something "near," with the "practical" windows dear to their hearts; it was necessary to have special hardware made, as there was none to be had this side of England.

1908a

Machine resources were then so little understood that extensive drawings had to be made merely to show the mill man what to leave off. But the trim finally became only flat, narrow, horizontal wood bands around the room, one at the top

of windows and doors and another next to the floor, both connected with similar vertical wood bands to divide the walls smoothly and flatly into folded color planes; the trim merely completing window and door openings. When the interior had thus become wholly plastic, a new element entered architecture, strangely enough, an element that had not existed in architectural history before. Not alone in the trim but in numerous ways too tedious to describe in words, this revolutionary sense of the plastic whole, an instinct with me at first, began to work more

1931b and more intelligently and have fascinating, unforeseen consequences.

A new sense of repose in flat planes and quiet streamline effects had thereby and then found its way into building, as we can now see it admirably in steamships, airplanes and motor cars. The age came into its own and the age did not know its own. There had been nothing at all from overseas to help in getting this new architecture planted on American soil. From 1893 to 1910 these prairie houses had planted it there. Nothing from Japan had helped at all, except the marvel of Japanese color prints. They were a lesson in elimination of the insignificant and

1936a in the beauty of the natural use of materials.

Around 1909, Kuno Francke, German exchange Professor of Esthetics at Harvard, heard of those Prairie Houses and he came to investigate. He saw one and got my name as the architect; he saw another and got the same name. Finally he came to the Oak Park studio and stayed three days. He felt something was being created which was being wasted on my country and he tried to persuade me to go to Germany. He told me Germany was ready for what I had. But I had no intention of going: I didn't speak German and I wasn't sure I wanted to work for the Germans. I liked my own people.

But nine months later the Wasmuth publishing house said they wanted to publish all my work if I would come to supervise it. The portfolio appeared in

1953a 1910. It changed the course of architecture in Europe. Europe was ready for it.

By now I had committed the indiscretion that was eventually to leave me no peace and keep me from ever finding satisfaction in anything superficial. That

1936a indiscretion was a determination to search for the *qualities* in all things.

Larkin Company building, Buffalo, N. Y., 1904

THE DESTRUCTION OF THE BOX

I think I first *consciously* began to try to beat the box in the Larkin Building—1906. I found a natural opening to the liberation I sought when (after a great struggle) I finally pushed the staircase towers out from the corners of the main building, made them into free-standing, individual features. Then the thing began to come through as you may see.

I had *felt* this need for features quite early in my architectural life. You will see this feeling growing up, becoming more apparent a little later in Unity Temple:

"Unity Temple is where I thought I had it"
Unity Church, Oak Park, Ill., 1906

there perhaps is where you will find the first real expression of the idea that the space within the building is the reality of that building. Unity Temple is where I thought I had it, this idea that the reality of a building no longer consisted in the walls and roof. So that sense of freedom began which has come into the architecture of today for you and which we call organic architecture.

You may see, there in Unity Temple, how I dealt with this great architectural problem at that time. You will find the sense of the great room coming through—space not walled in now but more or less free to appear. In Unity Temple you will find the walls actually disappearing; you will find the interior space opening to the outside and see the outside coming in. You will see assembled about this interior space, screening it, various free, related features instead of enclosing walls. See, you now can make features of many types for enclosure and group the features about interior space with no sense of *boxing* it. But most important, after all, is the sense of shelter extended, expanded overhead, and which gives the indispensable sense of protection while leading the human vision beyond the walls. That primitive sense of shelter is a quality architecture should always have. If in a building you feel not only protection from above, but liberation of interior to outside space (which you do feel in Unity Temple and other buildings I have built) then you have one important secret of letting the interior space come through.

Now I shall try to show you why organic architecture is the architecture of democratic freedom. Why? Well . . .

Here—say—is your box:

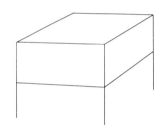

big hole in the box, little ones if you wish—of course.

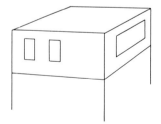

What you see of it now is this square package of containment. You see? Something not fit for our liberal profession of democratic government, a thing essentially anti-individual. Here you may see (more or less) the student architecture of almost all our colleges.

I was never ambitious to be an engineer. Unfortunately I was educated as one in the University of Wisconsin. But I knew enough of engineering to know that the outer angles of a box were not where its most economical support would be, if you made a building of it. No, a certain distance in each way from each corner

is where the economic support of a box-building is invariably to be found. You
see?

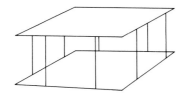

Now, when you put support at those points you have created a short
cantileverage to the corners that lessens actual spans and sets the corner free or
open for whatever distance you choose. The corners disappear altogether if you

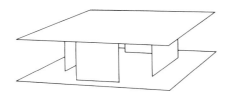

choose to let space come in there, or let it go out. Instead of post and beam construction, the usual box building, you now have a new sense of building construction
by way of the cantilever and continuity. Both are new structural elements as they
now enter architecture. But all you see of this radical liberation of space all over
the world today, is the corner window. But, in this simple change of thought lies
the essential of the architectural change from box to free plan and the new reality
that is *space* instead of matter.

From this point we can go on to talk about organic architecture instead of
classic architecture. Let's go on. These unattached side walls become something
independent, no longer enclosing walls. They're separate supporting screens, any
one of which may be shortened, or extended or perforated, or occasionally eliminated. These free-standing screens support the roof. What of this roof? Overhead

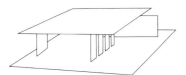

it becomes emphasized as a splendid sense of shelter, but shelter that hides nothing
when you are inside looking out from the building. It is a shape of shelter that
really gives a sense of the outside coming in or the inside going out. Yes, you have
now a wide-spreading overhead that is really a release of this interior space to the
outside: a freedom where before imprisonment existed.

You can perfect a figure of freedom with these four screens; in any case, enclosure as a box is gone. Anything becoming, anything in the nature of plan or materials is easily a possibility. To go further: if this liberation works in the horizontal plane why won't it work in the vertical plane? No one has looked through the box at the sky up there at the upper angle, have they? Why not? Because the

box always had a cornice at the top. It was added to the sides in order that the box might not look so much like a box, but more classic. This cornice was the feature that made your conventional box classic.

Now—to go on—there in the Johnson Building you catch no sense of enclosure whatever at any angle, top or sides. You are looking at the sky and feel the freedom of *space*. The columns are designed to stand up and take over the ceiling, the column is made a part of the ceiling: continuity.

The old idea of a building is, as you see, quite gone. Everything before these liberating thoughts of cantilever and continuity took effect, was post and beam construction: super-imposition of one thing upon another and repetition of slab over slab, always on posts. Now what? You have established a natural use of glass according to this new freedom of space. Space may now go out or come in where

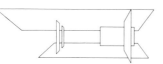

life is being lived, space as a component of it. So organic architecture is architecture in which you may feel and see all this happen as a third dimension. Too bad the Greeks didn't know of this new use for steel and glass as a third dimension. If they had known what I am trying to describe here, you wouldn't have to think much about it for yourselves today, the schools would long ago have taught these principles to you.

Be that as it may, this sense of space (space alive by way of the third dimension), isn't that sense, or *feeling* for architecture, an implement to characterize the freedom of the individual? I think so. If you refuse this liberated sense of building haven't you thrown away that which is most precious in our own human life and

"The destruction of the box"
Detail, Bach house, Chicago, Ill., 1915

most promising as a new field for truly creative artistic expression in architecture? Yes, is there anything else, really? All this, and more, is why I have, lifelong, been fighting the pull of the specious old *box*. I have had such a curious, controversial and interesting time doing it that I myself have become a controversial item. Suspicion is always in order.

Now, to go back to my own experiences: after this building of Unity Temple (as I have said) I thought I had the great thing very well in hand. I was feeling somewhat as I imagine a great prophet might. I often thought, well, at least here is an essentially new birth of thought, feeling and opportunity in this machine age. This is the modern means. *I* had made it come true! Naturally (I well remember) I became less and less tolerant and, I suppose, intolerable. Arrogant, I imagine, was the proper word. I have heard it enough.

Well, something always happens when you are arrogant out of proportion.

One day I went to my study at Taliesin to sit down and rest. I picked up a little book just received from the ambassador to America from Japan. It was called *The Book of Tea* written by Okakura Kakuzo. I wonder how many of you have read it? Well, in that little book I came upon quotations from the great Chinese poet-prophet Laotze, things he had said five hundred years before Jesus. As I turned the pages I suddenly came across this: "The reality of the building does not consist in the four walls and the roof but in the space within to be lived in." Strange! Never had I seen it before. I could scarcely believe my eyes and reread it several times.

Well ... well ... for a day or two I walked about disillusioned of my former self: felt something like a sail looks when coming down. Then, being well, I began to think again. I thought ... now ... wait a minute: Laotze *said* it. Yes. But, I built it. Then I began to come up again to former size and have been doing quite well ever since, arrogance unimpaired—thank you.

1952a

(Mr. Wright held up a water glass.)

Where *does* reality come in here? In the glass, in *this?* No! With the lesson in mind I've just given you, you should see the answer. You do see, don't you? Well —now just what *is* reality here in this so familiar object we call a drinking glass? The answer is, reality is the space within into which you can put something. In other words, the *idea.* And so it is with architecture; so it is with your lives; and so it is with everything you can *experience* as reality. You will soon find out for yourselves if you begin to work with this principle in mind, that things will open to you. They will develop you and to you. You will soon see that so many "grapes of wrath" have grown where none need have grown. Therein lies the secret of great *peace,* missing in our Western civilization today.

1914a

If I had a right to project myself in the direction of an organic architecture twenty-one years ago, it entailed the right to my work and, so far as I am able, a right to defend my aim. Also, yet not so clearly, I am bound to do what I can to save the public from untoward effects that follow in the wake of my own break with traditions. I deliberately chose to break with traditions in order to be more true to tradition than current conventions and ideals in architecture would permit. The more vital course is usually the rougher one and lies through conventions oftentimes settled into laws that must be broken, with consequent liberation of other forces that cannot stand freedom. So a break of this nature is a thing dangerous, nevertheless indispensable, to society.

... The principles of construction that made the countenance of that architecture what it was, seem never to have been grasped. Louis Sullivan ("Lieber Meister") and I used to talk of it as organic, and this concept of architecture—both ridiculed and admired—was the result of these principles.

Organic architecture is distinguished from the façade-making which passes for modern architecture today, as you can see in our home, Taliesin West. Organic architecture believes in the destruction of what the so-called International Style has maintained as the box. We had a feeling that since the nature of modern life

Taliesin West, Scottsdale, Ariz., 1938

"Man could look out of the corner where he had never looked before"
Fallingwater, Bear Run, Pa., 1936

was marked by its profession of freedom, there should be a free expression in building. The box was merely an inhibition and a constraint. All architecture had been the box—a decorated box, or a box with its lid exaggerated, or a box with pilasters, but always a box.

And the box did not fulfill the possibilities of steel and glass. Steel—the new material—allowed tenuity. Now you could make the building tough with tensile strength. If the idea was to do away with the box, here was the means.

There now came the cantilever. You could put the load under the center of the beam or you could reduce the span between the corners by moving the supports inward and leaving the corner open. In that single circumstance—what I suppose would be called engineering—came the opportunity to destroy the box. Now the walls could be merely screens and the corners could be knocked out. Man could look out of the corner where he had never looked before.

What could happen horizontally could also happen to the vertical. The essential nature of the box could be eliminated. Walls could be screens independent of each

"The essential nature of the box could be eliminated"
S. C. Johnson and Son administration building, Racine, Wis., 1936

"Interior space comes free"
S. C. Johnson and Son
administration building, Racine,
Wis., 1936

other; the open plan appeared naturally; the relationship of inhabitants to the outside became more intimate; landscape and building became one, more harmonious; and instead of a separate thing set up independently of landscape and site, the building with landscape and site became inevitably one. So the life of the individual was broadened and enriched by the new concept of architecture, by light and freedom of space.

But instead of understanding the principle involved in organic architecture, what went around the world was the corner window and the cantilever—without any sense of the release of space which had inspired them. Architects who thought they were modern, concentrated on the box and the exposure of structure. Why should you always expose structure? I call it "indecent exposure." 1953a

I began as a young architect-engineer. When I looked at the hideous efflorescent boxing in of humanity upon the Chicago prairies of the '90s, I soon realized that the corners of the box were not economical or vital bearing points of structure. The main load of the usual building, I saw, was on the walls and so best supported at points some distance back from the corner. Spans were then reduced by cantileverage. So I took the corners out, put in glass instead: the corner window. I gave a real blow here to all boxing up or boxing in. With the bearing points thus drawn in and clearly established aside from the corners, another result was that walls themselves became individual screens for interior space. Space could now be handled freely to bring in or shut out the out-of-doors at will. This much was for 1951a the ground plan. In the Johnson Building came the first time I had the nerve to knock the enclosing angle out between wall and ceiling. I thought if it works in one plane of the room, why won't it work as well (or better) up there. And it did work another miracle. When you go into the Johnson Building interior space comes free, you're not aware of any boxing in at all. Restricted space simply isn't there. Right there where you've always experienced this interior constriction you 1953b take a look at the sky!

Making away with the box both in plan and elevation now became fundamental to my work. That opened the way for feeling the space within as the Reality of all true modern building, building not merely monumental. I have sought this liberation in some form or other in almost every building I have built.... 1951a These structures now bear the message of this liberation of space to space.

EXTERIOR EFFECTS

... Young critics, I believe, intrigued by the science and philosophy of the great art, love architecture as a mysterious essence. They see in the surface and mass abstractions by "great and gifted" Europeans, inspired by French painting, the truth. But I know these abstractions repudiate the third dimension, ignoring depth of matter to get surface effects characteristic of canvas and pigment, as painting, but not of architecture no matter howsoever stark or begot by gas pipe, thin slabs, and naked steel work. Materials may now be used as decorative clichés too, witness the concoctions of wire, lead pipe, plumbing fittings, brass keys, bits of glass and wood, of this school. Sophisticated, ingenious, cleverly curious, they smell of the dissecting room, affect me as cadavers. . . .

These walls artificially thin, like cardboard bent and glued together. . . .   1929a

A plain flat surface cut to shape for its own sake, however large or plain the shape, is, the moment it is sophisticatedly so cut, no less ornamental than egg and dart. All buildings with such devices are objectionably ornamental, because like any buildings of the old classical order both wholly ignore the nature of integrity. Both also ignore modern resources and both neglect the nature of machines at work on materials. Incidentally and as a matter of course both misjudge the nature of time, place and the modern life of man.   1943a

Proportion is nothing in itself. It is a matter of relation to environment modified always by every feature, exterior as well as interior. Le Corbusier, hard as nails and sane as a hammer up to this point, goes as superstitious as a milkmaid lost in the mist of a moonlit night.   1932b

. . . The proper scale for a building is the human being, the human scale. "Grandomania," as I called it then and still do, seemed intended to give man an inferiority complex; monumentality was devised so he could be reduced by the systems of authority.   1953a

Our architecture itself would become a poor, flat-faced thing of steel bones, box outlines, gas pipe and handrail fittings—as sun-receptive as a concrete sidewalk or a glass tank without essential *heart* beating in it. Architecture, without it, could inspire nothing, and would degenerate to a box merely to *contain* objets d'art—objects which properly it should itself create and *maintain.* So beware! The artist who condemns romance is only a foolish reactionary. Such good sense as the scientist or philosopher disguised as artist may have is not creative, although it may be corrective. Listen therefore and go back with what you may learn, to live and be true to romance.   1931b

THE ARCHITECT'S LIMITATIONS

. . . Architecture which is really architecture proceeds from the ground and somehow the terrain, the native industrial conditions, the nature of materials and the purpose of the building, must inevitably determine the form and character of any good building.   1939a

An axiom: the solution of every problem is contained within itself. Its plan, form and character are determined by the nature of the site, the nature of the materials used, the nature of the system using them, the nature of the life concerned and the purpose of the building itself. And always a qualifying factor is the nature 1937c of the architect himself.

Well, architecture today is a great orchestration of materials, methods, and men. The architect must be correlated to it all, but he must also rise above it all. When he does so, machine conditions will only have extended his opportunities, 1930b however he may choose to divide his responsibilities. . . .

THE ARCHITECT AND "THE SYSTEM"

It is seldom that collaboration can enter into truly creative work except as one man conceives and another executes. But, even so, the highest is not attained that way. In the art of architecture conception and execution should be a self-contained unit. An architect's assistants should be like the fingers on his hands in relation to the work he is to do. The committee meeting at best never produced anything in architecture above the level of a compromise. Nor has a public architectural competition ever resulted in anything above the averaging of averages. Competitions 1937c are devastating where creative work is concerned.

Political or established Authority, I have observed in my lifetime, is, and so 1932a soon, the enemy of all validity.

Instinctively all forms of pretense fear and hate reality.

THE HYPOCRITE MUST ALWAYS HATE THE RADICAL.

Mr. Wright and his apprentices, 1938

ARCHITECT AND CLIENT

No man can build a building for another who does not believe in him, who does not believe in what he believes in, and who has not chosen him because of this faith, knowing what he can do. That is the nature of architect and client as I see it. When a man wants to build a building he seeks an interpreter, does he not? He seeks some man who has the technique to express that thing which he himself desires but cannot do. So, should a man come to me for a building, he would be ready for me. It would be, what I could do, that he wanted.   1939a

But the architect with the ideal of an organic architecture at stake can talk only principle and sense. His only appeal is fresh and must be made to the independent thought and judgment of his client such as it is. The client, too, must know how to think a little or follow from generals to particulars. How rare it is for an architect to go into any court where that quality of mind is on the bench! This architect has learned to dread the personal idiosyncrasy—offered him three times out of five—as a substitute for the needed, hoped-for intelligence.   1932a

Plastered houses were then new. Casement windows were new. So many things were new. Nearly everything was new but the law of gravity and the idiosyncrasy of the client.   1936a

TWO WAYS TO SEE A HOUSE

Any house is a far too complicated, clumsy, fussy, mechanical counterfeit of the human body. Electric wiring for nervous system, plumbing for bowels, heating system and fireplaces for arteries and heart, and windows for eyes, nose and lungs generally. The structure of the house, too, is a kind of cellular tissue stuck full of bones, complex now as the confusion of bedlam and all beside. The whole interior is a kind of stomach that attempts to digest objects—objets d'art maybe, but objects always. There the affected affliction sits, ever hungry—for ever more objects—

or plethoric with over plenty. The whole life of the average house, it seems, is a sort of indigestion. A body in ill repair, suffering indisposition—constant tinkering and doctoring to keep alive. It is a marvel, we its infestors do not go insane in it and with it. Perhaps it is a form of insanity we have put into it. Lucky we are able to get something else out of it, though we do seldom get out of it alive ourselves.

1931b

Taliesin, Spring Green, Wis., 1925

A house, we like to believe, can be a noble consort to man and the trees; therefore the house should have repose and such texture as will quiet the whole and make it graciously at one with external nature.

1931b

Guest room terrace, Fallingwater, Bear Run, Pa., 1939

"Graciously at one with external nature"
Entrance, Fallingwater, Bear Run, Pa., 1936

THE SANITARY SLUM

Along with this modernistic myopia picturesque skyscraper confusion worse confounded, there now goes the vexing problem of the tenement. This extensive, would-be beneficent, government housing of the poor. Yes, the poor are not only to be with us always, but the poor are to be recognized and multiplied per se as such. And so, multiplied officially too, they are to be built in as official fixture of the cities of the great free United States of America. Yes . . . the poor are to be so poor as to be accepted, confirmed and especially provided for as inevitable factors therein. As seen in any federal plan, catastrophe is to be made organic. The poor are to be built in!

Yes, the slums of today are to be made into the slums of tomorrow.

That the poor will benefit by increased sanitation may be granted at a glance. Not only are the living quarters of the poor to be more germ-proof, but where individual choice is concerned life itself is rendered antiseptic. If we trust our eyes.

Skyscrapers are let down sidewise as traps to crucify, not liberate, humanity. And the poor man's life is to become just as the rich man's office—No. 36722, block 99, shelf 17, entrance K, with a few twists and turns thrown in to distract attention from the fact. The poor man gets a bathtub and a flower box, a patch of lawn, but what freedom to say, and believe what he says, were he to say his soul is his own?

Surface-and-mass architecture thus extinguishes the poor man as it has already distinguished his landlord: therefore why should the poor man complain? Has the poor man not still his labor for his pains? And what has the rich man for his, I ask you? Ask him.

Yes, there he is, the poor man! No longer in a rubbish heap. No.   1932a

PRELIMINARY

The country between Madison and Janesville, near Taliesin my home and work-shop, is the bed of an ancient glacier drift. Vast busy gravel pits abound there, exposing heaps of yellow aggregate once and still everywhere near, sleeping beneath the green fields. Great heaps, clean and golden, are always waiting there in the sun. And I never pass on my way to and from Chicago without an emotion, a vision of the long dust-whitened stretches of the cement mills grinding to impalpable fineness the magic powder that would "set" my vision all to shape; I wish both mill and gravel endlessly subject to my will.

Nor do I ever come to a lumber yard with its citylike, graduated masses of fresh shingles, boards and timbers, without taking a deep breath of its fragrance, seeing the forest laid low in it by processes that cut and shaped it to the architect's scale of feet and inches, coveting it all.

The rock ledges of a stone quarry are a story and a longing to me. There is a suggestion in the strata, and character in the formation. I like to sit and feel the stone as it is there. Often I have thought, were monumental great buildings ever given me to build I would go to the Grand Canyon of Arizona to ponder them.

When in early years I looked south from the massive stone tower in the Auditorium Building, a pencil in the hand of a master, the red glare of the Bessemer steel converters to the south of Chicago would thrill me as pages of the Arabian Nights used to do with a sense of terror and romance.

And the smothered incandescence of the kiln: in the fabulous heat, mineral and chemical treasure baking on mere clay, to issue in all the hues of the rainbow, all the shapes of imagination that never yield to time, subject only to the violence or carelessness of man. These great ovens would cast a spell upon me as I listened to the subdued roar deep within them.

The potter's thumb and finger deftly pressing the soft mass whirling on his wheel as it yielded to his touch, the bulbous glass at the end of the slender pipe as the breath of the glass blower and his deft turning decided its shape—its fate fascinated me. Something was being born.

Colors; in paste or crayon, pencil; always a thrill. To this day I love to hold a handful of many-colored pencils and open my hand to see them lying loose upon my palm, in the light.

Mere accidental colored chalk marks on the sunlit sidewalk, perhaps, will make me pause and something in me harks back to something half remembered, half felt, and as though an unseen door had opened and distant music had, for an instant, come trembling through to my senses.

In this sense of earth!—deep-buried treasure there without end. Mineral matter and metal stores folded away in veins of gleaming quartz. Gold and silver, lead and copper, tawny iron ore; all will yield themselves up to roaring furnaces and flow obedient to the hands of the architect; all become pawns to human will in the plan of the human mind.

And jewels, happy discoveries. The gleam of mineral colors and flashing facets of crystals. Gems to be sought and set; to forever play with light to man's delight, in never-ending beams of purest green, or red or blue or yellow, and all that lives between. Light! Living in the mathematics of form to match with the mathematics of sound.

Crystals are proof of nature's matchless architectural principle.

All this I see as the architect's garden, his palette. . . .

'Materials! What a resource.

1928g

Midway Gardens, Chicago, Ill., 1914

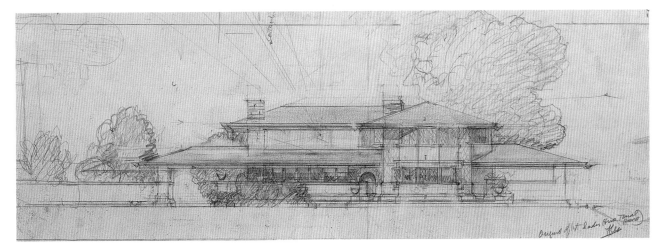

"A Home in a Prairie Town," *Ladies' Home Journal*, Curtis Publishing Co., New York, N.Y., 1901: project

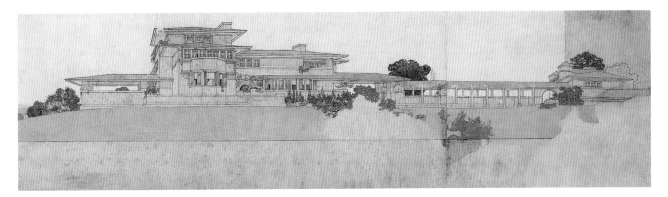

Metzger house, Sault Ste. Marie, Mich., 1902: project

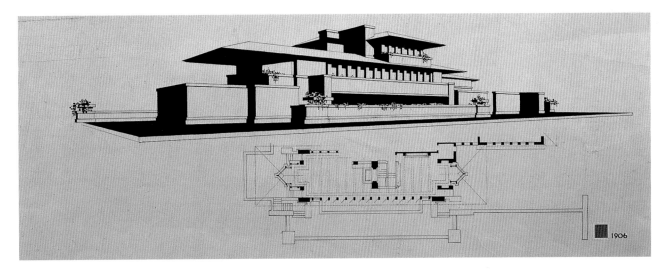

Robie house, Chicago, Ill., 1906

Gale house, Oak Park, Ill., 1909

Bach house, Chicago, Ill., 1915

Millard house, "La Miniatura," Pasadena, Cal., 1923

Hanna house, "Honeycomb House," Stanford, Cal., 1935

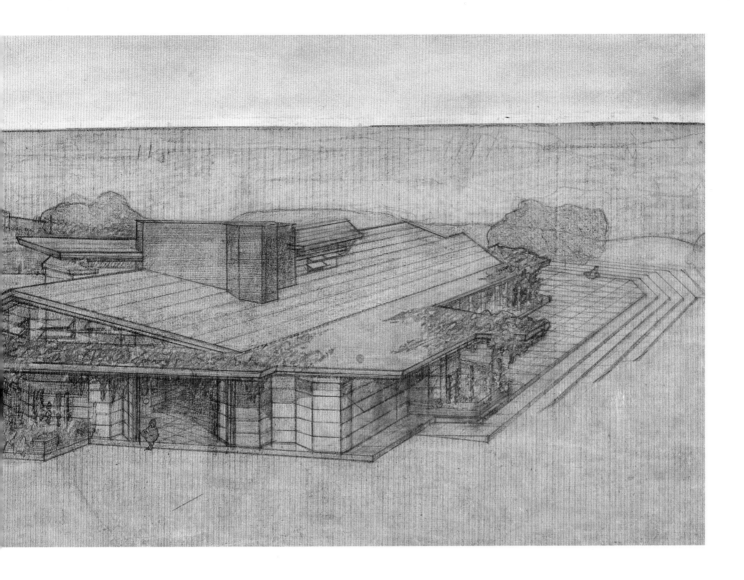

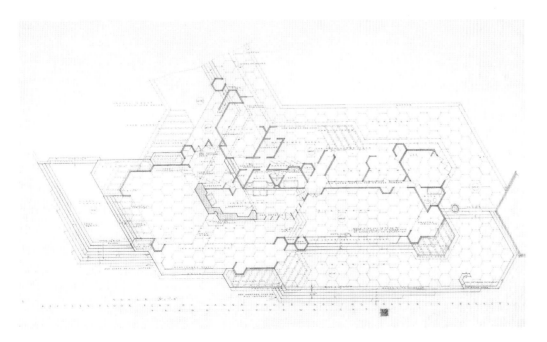

Floorplan, Hanna house

Perspective and floor plan, Jester house, Palos Verdes, Cal., 1938: project

ERIC BASS COURT CENTER FOR NINA G. ANDERTON
BEVERLY HILLS, CALIFORNIA
FRANK LLOYD WRIGHT ARCHITECT

Anderton Court shops, Beverly Hills, Cal., 1952

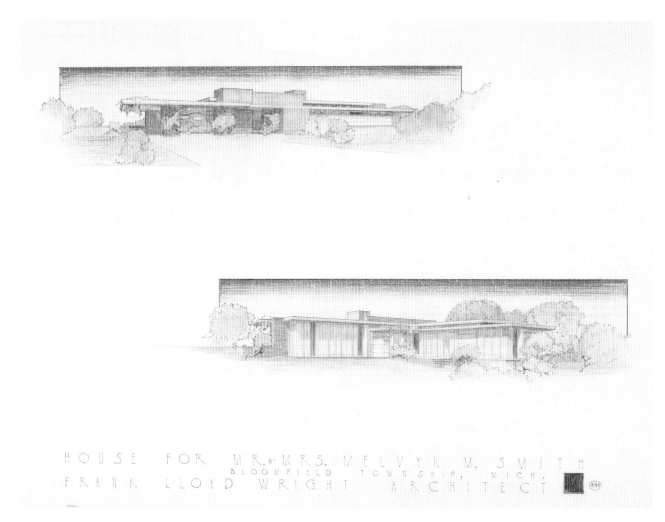

Two perspectives, Smith house, Bloomfield Hills, Mich., 1946

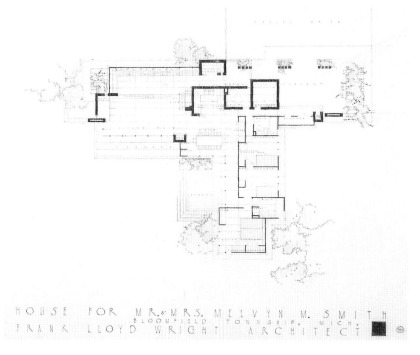

Floorplan, Smith house

S. C. Johnson & Son Company research laboratory, Racine, Wis., 1944

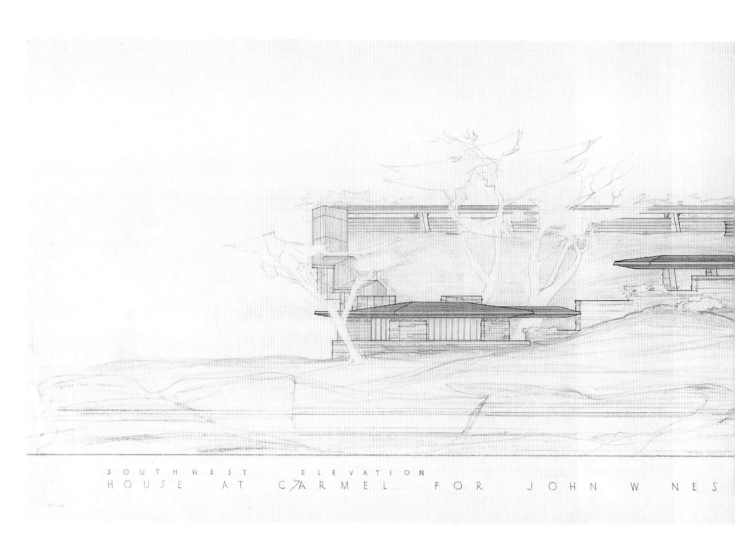

SOUTHWEST ELEVATION
HOUSE AT CARMEL FOR JOHN W NES

Nesbitt house, "Sea Garden," Carmel, Cal., 1940: project

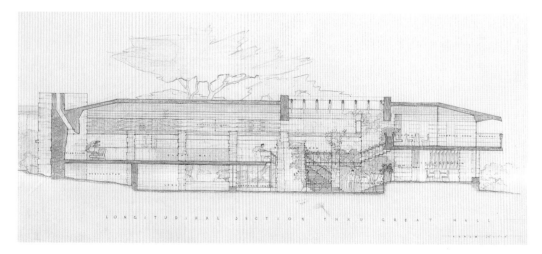

LONGITUDINAL SECTION THRU GREAT HALL

Section, Nesbitt house

ITT   F R A N K   L L O Y D   W R I G H T   A R C H I T E C T

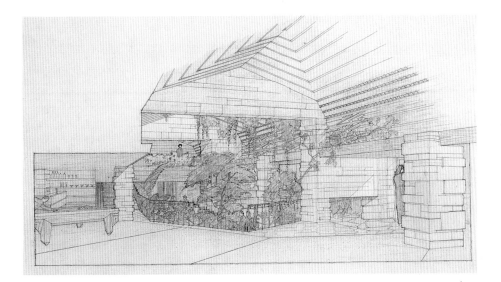

Living room, Nesbitt house

Guggenheim Museum, New York, N.Y., 1943

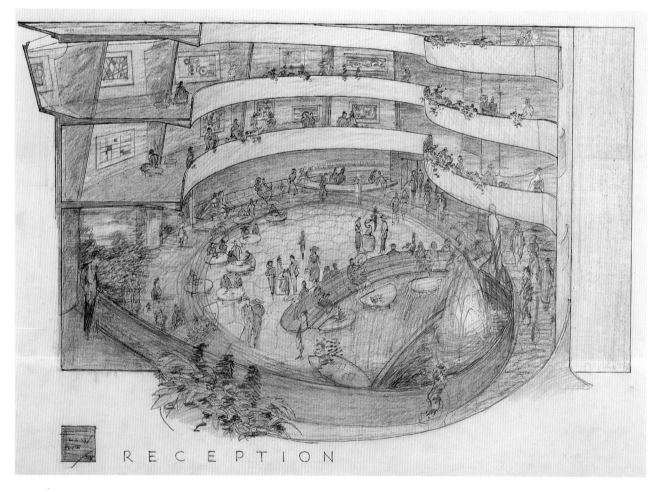

RECEPTION

Interior perspective, Guggenheim Museum

VIEW FROM NORTHEAST
POINT VIEW RESIDENCES
FOR THE EDGAR J. KAUFMANN CHARITABLE TRUST
FRANK LLOYD WRIGHT ARCHITECT

"Point View Residences," apartment tower, scheme #1, Pittsburgh, Pa., 1952: project

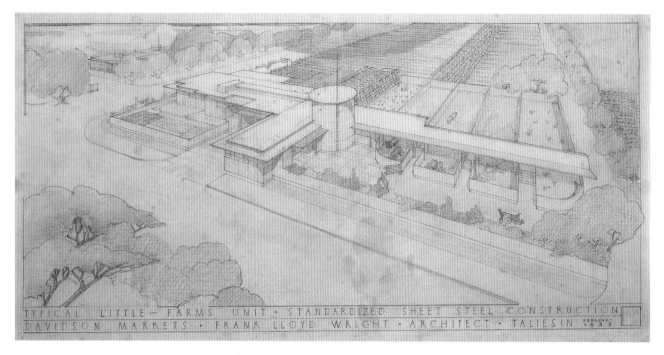

Prefabricated Sheet Metal farm units, 1932: project

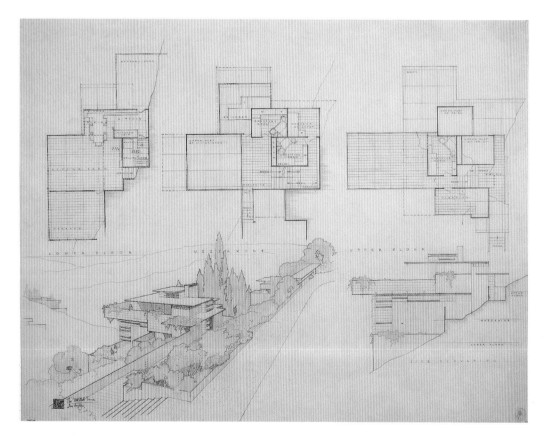

All Steel houses, Los Angeles, Cal., 1938: project

OFFICE BUILDING FOR NATIONAL LIFE INSURANCE CO. OF U.S.A. CHICAGO · A.M.JOHNSON PRESIDENT · FRANK LLOYD WRIGHT ARCHITECT

National Life Insurance Company building, Chicago, Ill., 1924: project

THE GOLDEN BEACON
CHICAGO ILLINOIS
FRANK LLOYD WRIGHT ARCHITECT

"Golden Beacon," apartment tower, Chicago, Ill., 1956: project

"New machine age resources require that all buildings not resemble each other"

Above, Taliesin West, Scottsdale, Ariz., 1936

Below, C. R. Wall house, Plymouth, Mich., 1941

Preliminary version, The Guggenheim Museum, New York, N. Y., project begun 1943

V. C. Morris shop, San Francisco, Cal., 1947

Now there can be nothing frozen or static about either the methods or effects of organic architecture. All must be the spontaneous reaction of the creative mind 1951a to a specific problem in the nature of materials.

To be modern simply means that all materials are used honestly for the sake 1931a of their own qualities, and that the materials modify the design of the building.

New machine-age resources require that all buildings not resemble each other; the new ideal does not require that all buildings be of steel, concrete or glass: often that might be idiotic waste.

Nor do our present-day resources imply that mass is no longer a beautiful attribute of masonry, when genuinely used. We are entitled to a vast variety of form in our complex age so long as the form be genuine—serves architecture while architecture serves life.

But in this land of ours, richest on earth in old and new materials, the architect must exercise well-trained imagination to see in each material, either natural or compounded, its own inherent style. All materials may be beautiful, their beauty 1932a depending much or entirely upon how well they are used by the architect.

It takes creative imagination to see stone as Stone; see steel as Steel; see glass as Glass, and to view traditions as Tradition.

1930a

Preliminary version, Masieri Memorial, Venice, Italy, 1953

I began to learn to see brick as Brick. I learned to see wood as Wood and learned to see concrete or glass or metal each for itself and all as themselves. Strange to say, this required uncommon sustained concentration of uncommon imagination (we call it vision); it demanded not only a new conscious approach to building but opened a new world of thought that would certainly tear down the old world completely. Each different material required a different handling, and each different handling as well as the material itself had new possibilities of use peculiar to the nature of each. Appropriate designs for one material would not be at all appropriate for any other material.... All materials modify if indeed they do not create the form when used with understanding according to the limitations of process and purpose.

1936a   Architecture might, and did, begin life anew.

LIGHT

More and more, light began to become the beautifier of the building—the blessing of the occupants. Our arboreal ancestors in their trees are more likely precedent for us than the savage animals that holed in for protection. Yes, in a spiritual sense, a higher *order* is the sense of sunlit space and the lightness of the structure of the spider spinning, as John Roebling saw it and realized it in his
1931c   Brooklyn Bridge.

Shadows were the brushwork of the ancient architect. Let the modern now work with light, light diffused, light reflected, light refracted—light for its own
1931b   sake, shadows gratuitous.

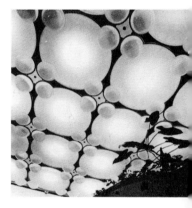

Ceiling, V. C. Morris shop, San Francisco, Cal., 1947

Lighting may be made a part of the building itself. No longer any appliance
1928c   or even appurtenance are needed. But all this may be made, really, architecture.

Proper orientation of the house, then, is the first condition of the lighting of that house; and artificial lighting is nearly as important as daylight. Daylighting can be beautifully managed by the architect if he has a feeling for the course of the sun as it goes from east to west and at the inevitable angle to the south. The sun is the great luminary of all life. It should serve as such in the building of any house. There is, however, the danger of taking light too far and leaving the inmate defenseless in a glass cage—which is somewhat silly. You must control light in the

planning of your home so that light most naturally serves your needs without too much artificial production and consequent control—putting light in only to block it out.

As for all artificial lighting, it too should be integral part of the house—be as near daylighting as possible. In 1893, I began to get rid of the bare light bulb and have ever since been concealing it on interior decks or placing it in recesses in such a way that it comes from the building itself; the effect should be that it comes from the same source as natural light.

1954a

Two views of Taliesin West, Scottsdale, Ariz., 1938

Larkin Company building, Buffalo, N. Y., 1904

S. C. Johnson and Son research center, Racine, Wis., 1947

GLASS

Glass has now a perfect visibility, thin sheets of air crystallized to keep air currents outside or inside. Glass surfaces, too, may be modified to let the vision sweep through to any extent up to perfection. Tradition left no orders concerning this material as a means of perfect visibility; hence the sense of glass as crystal has not, as poetry, entered yet into architecture.

1931b

S. C. Johnson and Son
administration building,
Racine, Wis., 1936

So let us now consider the new resource, glass. This resource is new and a "super-material" in modern life only because it holds such amazing means for awakened sensibilities. It amounts to a new qualification of life in itself. If known in ancient times glass would then and there have abolished the ancient architecture we know, and completely. This super-material GLASS as we now use it is a miracle: air in air, to keep air out or keep it in. Light itself in light, to diffuse or reflect, or refract light itself.

By means of glass, then, open reaches of the ground may enter into the building and the building interior may reach out and associate with these vistas of the ground. Ground and building will thus become more and more obviously directly related to each other in openness and intimacy; not only as environment but also as a good pattern for the good life lived in the building.

Perhaps more important than all beside, it is by way of glass that sunlit space as a reality becomes the most useful servant of the human spirit. Free living in air and sunlight aid cleanliness of form and idea; through glass this is coming in the new architecture. And the integral character of extended vistas gained by marrying buildings to ground levels, or blending them with slopes and gardens; yes, it is in this new sense of earth as a great human good that we will move forward in the building of our new homes and great public buildings.

1932a

The machine gives prismatic opportunity in glass. The machine process can do any kind of glass: thick, thin, colored, textured to order; and cheap; and the machine in the architect's hand can now set it, protect it, and humanize its use completely. . . .

1928c

. . . As glass has become clearer and clearer and cheaper and cheaper from age to age, about all that has been done with it architecturally is to fill with a perfect visibility now the same building openings that opaque, ill-made but beautiful glass screened long ago.

1928c

Entrance, S. C. Johnson and Son administration building, Racine, Wis., 1936

Glass detail, Fallingwater, Bear Run, Pa., 1936

Brickwork, S. C. Johnson and Son
administration building, Racine, Wis., 1936

BRICK

Make the walls of brick that the fire touched to tawny gold or ruddy tan, choicest of all earth's hues. They will not rise rudely above the sod . . . but recognize the surface of the ground on which they stand, gently spreading there to a substantial base that makes the building seem more firm in its earth-socket. Brick walls will carry with a profile of grace the protection of sheltering eaves.

1902a

WOOD

Wood is universally beautiful to man. It is the most humanly intimate of all materials. Man loves his association with it; likes to feel it under his hand, sympathetic to his touch and to his eye.

And yet, passing by the primitive uses of wood, getting to higher civilization, the Japanese understood it best. The Japanese have never outraged wood in their art or in their craft. Japan's primitive religion, Shinto, with its "be clean" ideal found in wood ideal material and gave it ideal use in that masterpiece of architecture, the Japanese dwelling, as well as in all that pertained to living in it.

In Japanese architecture may be seen what a sensitive material let alone for its own sake can do for human sensibilities, as beauty, for the human spirit.

Whether pole, beam, plank, board, slat, or rod, the Japanese architect got the forms and treatments of his architecture out of tree nature, wood wise, and heightened the natural beauty of the material by cunning peculiar to himself.

The possibilities of the properties of wood came out richly as he rubbed into it the natural oil of the palm of his hand, ground out the soft parts of the grain to leave the hard fiber standing, an "erosion" like that of the plain where flowing water washes away the sand from the ribs of the stone.

No Western people ever used wood with such understanding as the Japanese used it in their construction, where wood always came up and came out as nobly beautiful.

And when we see the bamboo rod in their hands, seeing a whole industrial world interpreting it into articles of use and art that ask only to be bamboo, we reverence the scientific art that makes wood theirs.

The simple Japanese dwelling with its fences and utensils is the revelation of wood.

1928d

Wood details, Shokintei Katsura Villa, ca. 1600

CONCRETE

Aesthetically concrete has neither song nor any story. Nor is it easy to see in this conglomerate, in this mud pie, a high aesthetic property, because in itself it is amalgam, aggregate compound. And cement, the binding medium, is characterless.   1928f

New life, new purposes and possibilities were given to both cement and steel when the coefficient of expansion and contraction was found to be the same in each. A new world was then and there opened to the architect.

What about the concrete block? It was the cheapest (and ugliest) thing in the building world. It lived mostly in the architectural gutter as an imitation of rock-faced stone. Why not see what could be done with that gutter rat? Steel rods cast inside the joints of the blocks themselves and the whole brought into some broad, practical scheme of general treatment, why would it not be fit for a new phase of our modern architecture? It might be permanent, noble, beautiful. It would be cheap.

All that imagination needed to make such a scheme feasible architecture was a plastic medium where steel would enter into inert mass as tensile strength. Concrete was the inert mass and would take compression. Concrete is a plastic material—susceptible to the impress of imagination. I saw a kind of weaving coming out of it. Why not weave a kind of building? Then I saw the shell. Shells with steel inlaid in them. Or steel for warp, and masonry units for woof in the weaving. For block-size—say units a man could handle weighing 40 to 50 pounds —all such blocks to be set steel-wound and steel-bound. Floors, ceilings, walls all the same—all to be hollow.

Lightness and strength! Steel the spider spinning a web within the cheap, molded material and wedded to it by pouring an inner core of cement after the blocks were set up.   1932a

...I finally had found simple mechanical means to produce a complete building that looks the way the machine made it, as much at least as any fabric need look. Tough, light, but not "thin"; imperishable; plastic; no unnecessary lie about it anywhere and yet machine-made, mechanically perfect. Standardization as the soul of the machine here for the first time may be seen in the hand of the architect, put squarely up to imagination, the limitations of imagination the only limitation of building.   1929a

Making concrete block for the Storer house, Los Angeles, Cal., 1923

Concrete block, Florida Southern College, Lakeland, Fla., begun 1938

Library building, Florida Southern College, Lakeland, Fla., begun 1938

David Wright house, Phoenix, Ariz., 1952

Administrative center, Florida Southern College,
Lakeland, Fla., begun 1938

Reinforced concrete, Price Tower, Bartlesville,
Okla., 1955

Sheet metal used at Price Tower, Bartlesville, Okla., 1955

SHEET METAL

What is left of the architectural framework of the modern world after concrete and steel have done with it will probably be in some form or other, sheet metal.

The machinery at work in the sheet metal trades easily crimps, folds, trims, and stamps sheets of metal as an ingenious child might his sheets of paper. The finished product may have the color brought up in surface treatment, or be enameled and colored with other durable substances, or as in galvanizing the finished work may be dipped and coated entire. But copper is the only sheet metal that has yet entered into architecture as beautiful permanent material. Its verdigris is always a great beauty in connection with stone or brick or wood, and copper is more nearly permanent than anything we have at hand as an architect's medium.

1928g

TALL BUILDINGS

In the steel and glass buildings I have designed, there are no walls, only wall-screens. The method of the cantilever in concrete and steel yields best to suspended screens or shells in place of outer walls; all may be shop-fabricated. The spider web is a good inspiration for steel construction. A slender mechanized fabric for all walls and partitions enters here to give the form and style that is architecture.

1928a

Chicago architects long before had discovered the possibility of using iron and steel to make a stone and brick building stand up so it could go on making masonry faces at admiring throngs all the way up, piling story on story. Of course, the tenuous open steel frame of these tall buildings is, in character, the reverse of oppressive masonry mass. Lightness, openness and tenuous strength combined are its building characteristics. These ought to be associated never with heavy stone or concrete but with light insulated covering: metal with glass insertions instead of heavy walls. The whole should be designed and insulated to emphasize the pattern of the structure itself with a fresh beauty not belying the way it was 1932a actually built.

These plans for the insurance building were opportunity to devise a more practical solution of the skyscraper problem than was current, because modern materials and methods add up advantages most heavily in their own favor where they can go farthest—either up and down or crosswise. Standardization in the nature of both sheet metal and reinforced concrete here might come completely into its own. Here, again the life of imagination must awaken life within the limitations of the architect's problem.

Now, exterior walls as such disappear—instead see suspended, standardized sheet-copper screens only slightly engaged at the edges of the floors. The walls

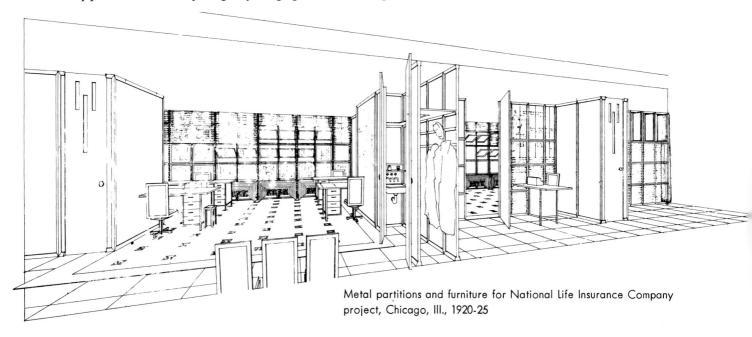

Metal partitions and furniture for National Life Insurance Company project, Chicago, Ill., 1920-25

themselves cease to exist either as weight or as thickness. Windows in this fabrication are a matter of units in a screen, opening singly or in groups at the will of the occupant. All the outside glass of the building may be cleaned from inside with neither bother nor risk. Vertical mullions (copper shells filled with nonconducting mastic) are large and strong enough only to carry from floor to floor. The mullions themselves project much or little, as more or less light is wanted. If much projection, the shadows are enriched; less projection dispels the shadows and brightens the interior. These projecting mullions are really vertical blades of copper, acting in the sun like the blades of a blind.

The unit of 2 feet both ways is small because the client seemed to have a fear of too much glass. In this instance the unit is emphasized on every alternate vertical with additional emphasis every fifth unit to increase the metal areas and create a larger rhythm. No emphasis is needed on the horizontal units; they would catch water or dust. The edges of the floors are beveled to the same dimension used between windows where engaged with all partitions, so floors appear in the screens merely as one of the horizontal divisions occurring regularly every 2 feet. The floors themselves however do appear at intervals in front of recessions in the surface screen, in order to bring the concrete structure itself into relief, in relation to the screen as well as in connection with it, thus weaving the two elements of structure together.

The outer building surfaces become opalescent, iridescent copper-bound glass. To avoid all interference with the light-giving exterior screen, supporting pylons are set back from the lot line, the floors carried by them thus becoming cantilever slabs. The extent of the cantilever, in this case 12 feet, is determined by the use for which the building is designed. The pylons are continuous through all floors and here are exposed at the top. The pylons are enlarged to carry electrical, plumbing, and heating conduits which branch from the shafts, not in the floor slabs but in piping designed as visible fixtures extending beneath the ceiling to where outlets are needed in each office. All electrical or plumbing appliances, free of the building in vertical shafts, may thus be disconnected and relocated at short notice with no waste in time or material.

Fabricated upon a unit system, the interior partitions may be made up in sections, complete with doors ready to set in place. Designed to match the general style of the outer wall-screen, these interior partitions may be stored ready to use; change to suit tenants could be made overnight with no waste. The client was an experienced landlord and these simples appealed to him. Again it was the kind of standardization that gave us the motor car, applied to building.

SECOND FLOOR

MEZZANINE

GROUND FLOOR

Section through and exterior of project for National Life Insurance Company, Chicago, Ill., 1920-25

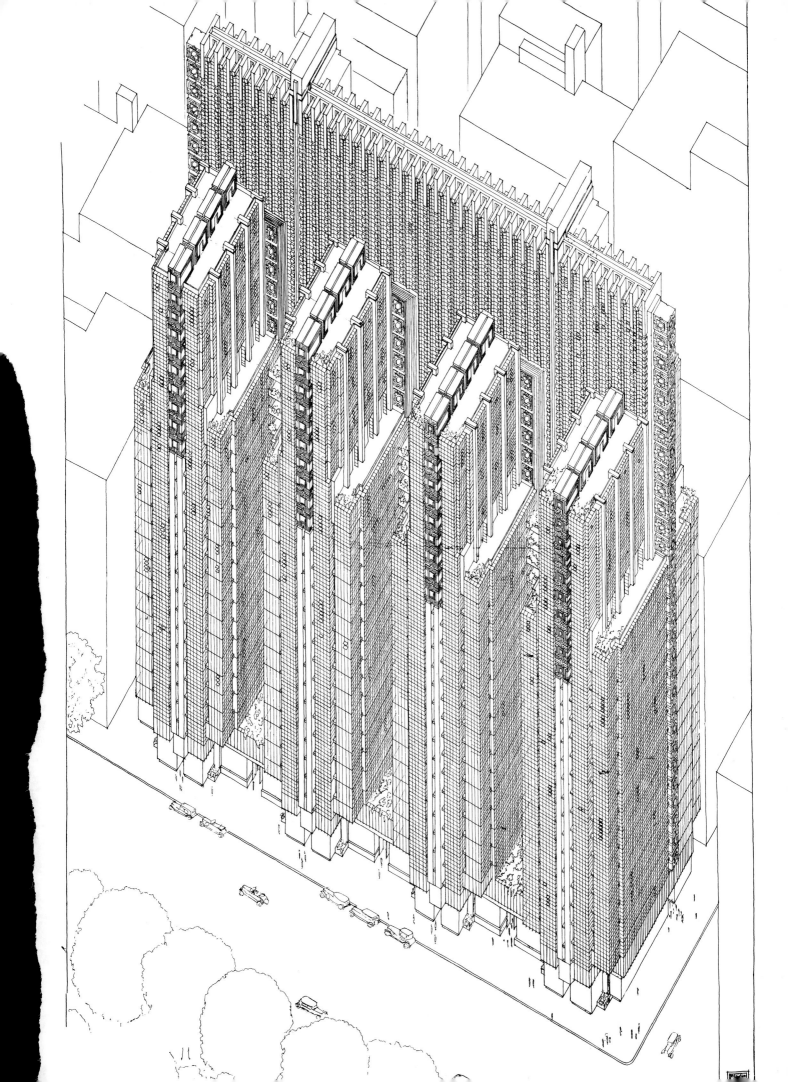

The increase of glass area over usual skyscraper fenestration is about 10 per cent (the margin could be increased or diminished by expanding or contracting the copper members in which the glass is set), so the heating expense is not much increased. The copper mullions are filled with insulating material and the window openings kept tight, thus the increase of glass is compensated. Radiators are cast as a railing set in front of the lower unit of this outer screen, free enough to make cleaning easy. For the first two stories or more unobstructed glass is suspended from the floor above, dreams of shopkeepers fully realized.

Connecting stairways necessary between floors are here arranged as practical fire escapes forming central features, seen at the front and rear of each section of the mass; and, though cut off by fireproof doors at each floor, the continuous stairway discharges upon the sidewalk below without obstruction.

The construction of such a building as this would be about one third lighter than anything in the way of a tall building yet built—and three times stronger in any disturbance. The construction is balanced as the human body on its legs, the walls hanging as the arms from the shoulders, the whole heavy only where weight insures stability.

Of chief value as I see it, the scheme as a whole legitimately eliminates masonry architecture that traditionally vexes such buildings. Architecture in this scheme now is become a shop fabrication. Only the most complicated part of the building need be assembled in the field.

The construction of pylons and floors is not involved with any interior or exterior surfaces. Indestructible, the fabric is made entirely independent of anything hitherto complicating it and mixed up with it.

Also piping and conduits for all appurtenances may be cut in the shop, the labor in the field reduced to assembling. No fitting; screwing up the joints is all that is necessary in either heating, lighting or plumbing.

Thus, literally, we have a shop-made building in all but the supporting posts and floors, which may be reinforced concrete or steel, concrete-masked in place. In this design architecture frankly, profitably and artistically—why not?—is taken from the field to the factory: the economic advantages are enormous and obvious.

There is no unsalable floor space in this building—no features inside or outside manufactured merely for architectural effect.

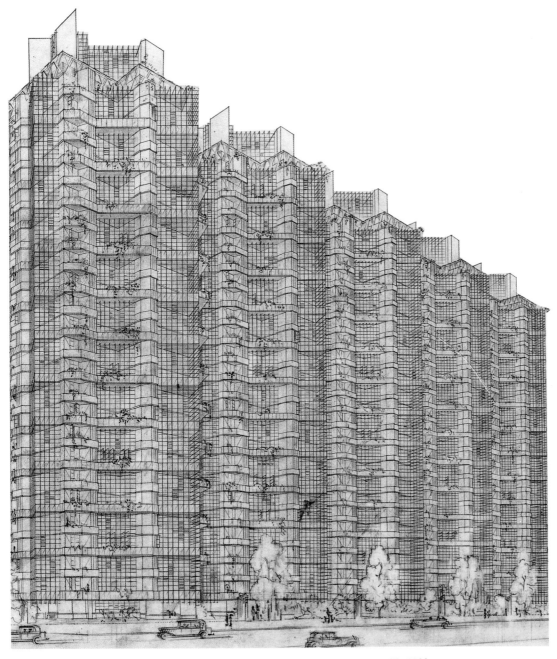

Above, perspective; below, plan at ground level: apartment project, Chicago, Ill., 1930

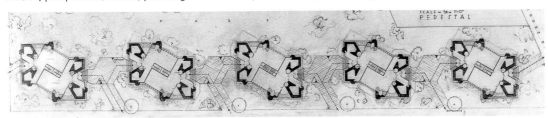

To gratify the landlord, his lot area now is salable to the very lot-line itself, and on every floor where ordinances do not demand they be reduced as the building soars upward.

Architecture here is a light, trim, practical commercial fabric—every inch and pound in service. There is every reason why it should be beautiful. But it was best to say nothing about that to the client; and I said very little about it.

The aim in this cantilever construction was to achieve scientific utility by means of the machine. To accomplish—first of all—a true standardization which would serve as the basis for me from which to project the whole, as an expression of principle, into a genuine living architecture of the present.

I began work on this study the winter of 1920, the main features of it having been in mind ever since the building of the Imperial in 1917. I had the good fortune to explain the scheme in detail and to show the developed preliminary drawings to Lieber Meister Louis H. Sullivan, shortly before he died. Gratefully I remember—and proudly—he said: "I had faith that it would come. It is a work of great art. I knew what I was talking about all these years—you see? I could never have done this building myself, but I believe that, but for me, you could never have done it."

I know I should never have reached it, but for what he was and what he himself did. This design is dedicated to him.

1932a

This skyscraper planned to stand free in an urban park and thus fit for human occupancy, is as nearly organic as steel in tension and concrete in compression can make it, doing for tall building what Lidgerwood made steel do for the long ship. The ship had its keel: this building has its concrete core. A shaft of concrete rises through the floors engaging each slab at eighteen levels. Each floor proceeds outward as a cantilever slab extended from the shaft. The slab, thick at the shaft, grows thinner as it goes outward in an overlapping scale pattern until at the final leap to the screen wall it is no more than 3 inches thick. The outer enclosing screen of glass and copper is pendent from these cantilever slabs; the inner partitions rest upon the slabs.

With four double-decked apartments to each floor, each apartment unaware of the other as all look outward, the structure eliminates the weight and waste

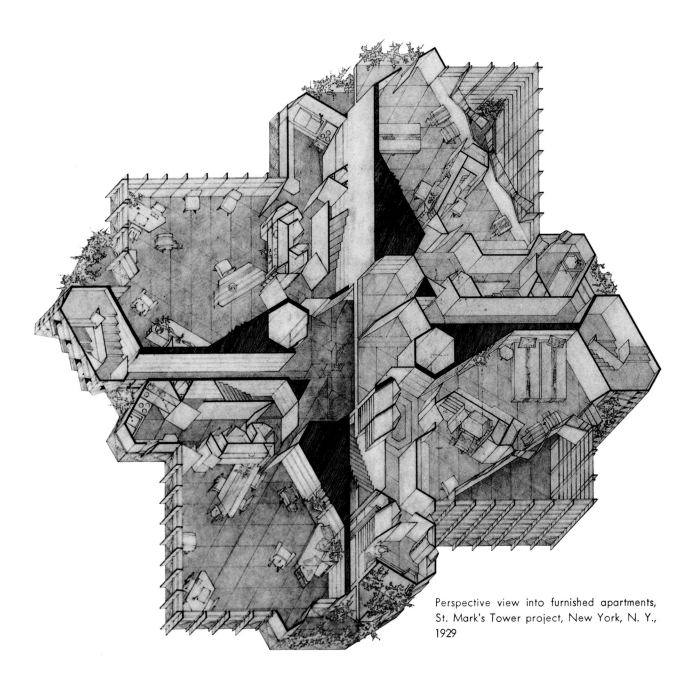

Perspective view into furnished apartments,
St. Mark's Tower project, New York, N. Y.,
1929

space of masonry walls. The central shaft standing inside, away from lighted space,
carries elevators and entrance hallway well within itself. Two of the exterior walls
of every apartment are entirely of glass set into sheet-copper framing. But the
building is so placed that the sun shines on only one wall at a time and narrow
upright blades, or mullions, project 9 inches so that as the sun moves, shadows
fall on the glass surfaces.

The building increases substantially in area from floor to floor as the structure rises, in order that the glass frontage of each story may drip clear of the one below, the building thus cleaning itself. Also, areas become more valuable the higher (within limits) the structure goes. The central shaft extending well into the ground may carry with safety a greatly extended top mass. This building, earthquake, fire and soundproof from within, by economics inherent in its structure weighs less than half the usual tall building and increases the area available for living by more than 20 per cent.

It is a logical development of the idea of a tall building in the age of glass and steel, as logical engineering as the Brooklyn Bridge or an ocean liner. But the benefits of modernity such as this are not merely economic. There is greater privacy, safety, and beauty for human lives within it than is possible in any other type of apartment building.

A one-two triangle is employed, because it allows flexibility of arrangement for human movement not afforded by the rectangle. The apparently irregular shapes of the rooms would not appear irregular in reality; all would have great repose because all are not only properly in proportion to the human figure but to the figure made by the whole building.

1938a

The building has a complete standardization for prefabrication; only the concrete core and slabs need be made in the field. Our shop-fabricating industrial system could function at its best here with substantial benefits to humanity. Owing to the unusual conformations the furniture would have to be a part of the building, as the metal (copper) furniture is designed to be. Here again is the poise, balance, lightness, and strength that may characterize the creations of this age.

The first expression of a treelike mast structure was in a project for St. Mark's-in-the-Bouwerie in 1929. The skyscraper was indeed the product of modern technology, but it was not suitable if it increased congestion, which it inevitably would unless it could stand free in the country. There was one planned as a feature of Broadacre City—so those from the city wouldn't feel lost in that vision of the country, and the Johnson laboratory tower is another such. But it was an idea that had to wait over thirty years for full realization. It is actually being built now by H. C. Price in Bartlesville, Okla. The total weight of the building will be about 6/10 of the conventional structure of the Rockefeller Center type, due to cantilever and continuity. Now the skyscraper will come into its own on the rolling plains of Oklahoma.

1953a

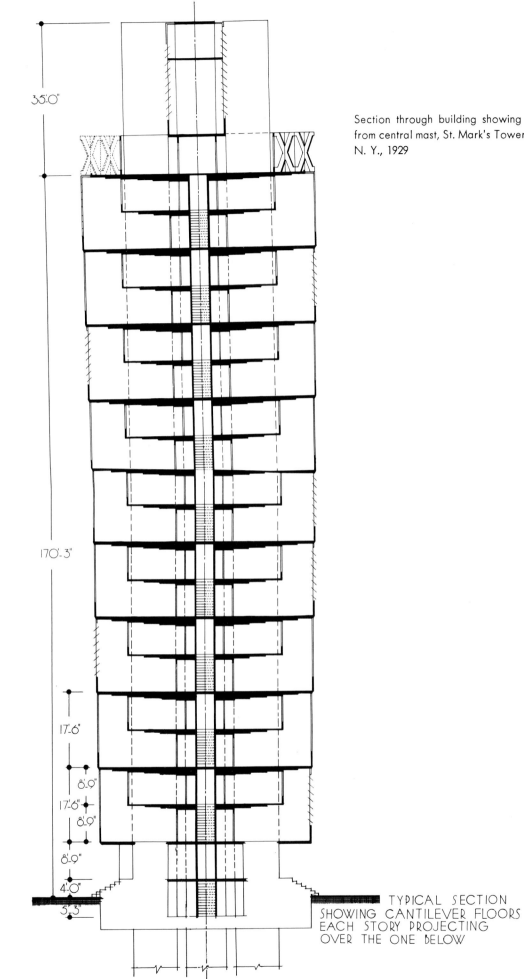

35'-0"

170'-3"

17'-6"

8'-9"

17'-6"

8'-9"

8'-9"

4'-0"

5'-3"

Section through building showing floors cantilevered from central mast, St. Mark's Tower project, New York, N. Y., 1929

TYPICAL SECTION
SHOWING CANTILEVER FLOORS
EACH STORY PROJECTING
OVER THE ONE BELOW

When the matter of a new research laboratory came up at the S. C. Johnson Wax Co., Herbert Johnson said, "Why not go up in the air, Frank?"

"That's just it," I said. I had seen several of the meandering, flat piles called laboratories, ducts running here, there and everywhere and a walkaround for everybody. I knew we would get twice the sunlight and twice the net working area, dollar for dollar, in a tall building.

So we went up in the air around a giant central stack with floors branching from it, having clear light and space all around each floor. All laboratory space was then clear and in direct connection with a duct-system cast in the hollow reinforced-concrete floors, connecting to the vertical hollow of the stack itself.

This seemed to me a natural solution . . . affording all kinds of delightful sunlit, directly related work space. Cantilevered from the giant stack, the floor slabs spread out like tree branches, providing sufficient segregation of departments vertically. Elevator and stairway channels up the central stack link these departments to each other. All utilities and the many intake and exhaust pipes run in their own central utility grooves, arranged like the cellular pattern of the tree trunk.

Glass tubes, S. C. Johnson and Son buildings, Racine, Wis., 1938-47

From each alternate floor slab an outer glass shell hangs firm. This glass shell, like that of the original administration building, is formed of glass tubes held in place by small vertical cast aluminum stanchions sealed horizontally by plastic. Inside, for temperature insurance, a second screen of plate glass was clipped to the aluminum stanchions and made movable for cleaning.

1951a

As skyscraperism characterizes the thought of the group characterizing the Chicago World's Fair—they themselves idealized the Fair as "New York seen from one of its own high buildings..."

Why not, then, the Fair itself apotheosis of the skyscraper?

Build a great skyscraper (in which the Empire State Building might stand free in a central court) devoted to all the resources of the modern elevator.

Instead of the old stage-props, the same old miles of picture-buildings faked in cheap materials, wrapped around a lagoon, a fountain or a theatrical waterfall—all to be eventually butchered—let there be, for once, a genuine modern construction.

If elevators handle the population of New York, they could handle the crowds at the Fair. Why not handle the crowds directly from several expansive tiers of mechanized parking space, great terraces from which the skyscraper itself would rise. The construction should be merely the steel itself designed as integral pattern in structural framing. Then concrete slabs for floors projecting as cantilever balconies, floor above floor—garden floors intervening as restaurants.

Instead of glass for enclosure—some light, transparent glass substitutes might be used; the multitudinous areas thus created would be let to exhibitors. The top stories could be garden observatories, pleasure places. A vast auditorium might join the skyscraper at the base to handle great aggregations of people on the ground. The tower construction might rise from triple-decked parking terraces, one corner of the terraces extending into the lake projecting two ways at right angles to make piers and harbors for water craft. Where the reflections of the tower would fall, powerful jets of the lake itself could be lifted by submerged power pumps to great height, all to be illuminated by modern light apparatus, projecting toward the tower and from it, the lake becoming thus at selected points a series of great fountains irradiated by light.

The Lake Front Park itself would be mere landscape adjunct to a great modern structure which might easily rise two hundred and forty-five stories, say two thousand five hundred feet above the lake level—or about a half mile high.

The clouds might naturally or artificially drift across its summit. Or effects be created by aeroplanes laying down colored ribbons of smoke to drift across it.

Such construction today would be no impossible feat, financially or structurally, in fact, entirely within reach.

126

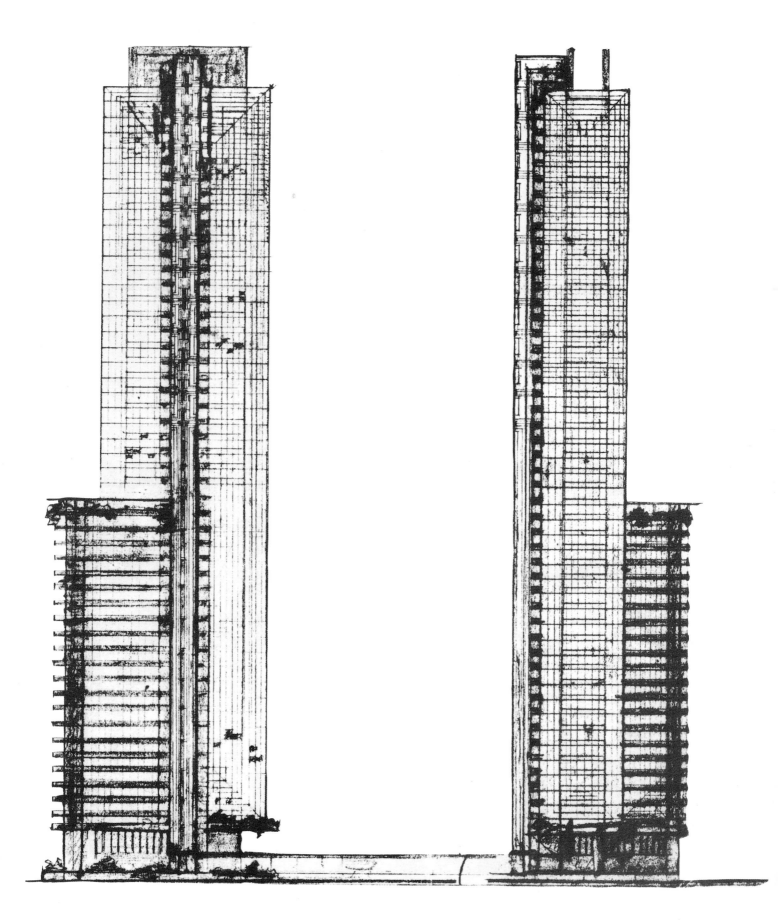

Sketches of front and side elevations
for skyscraper project, 1931

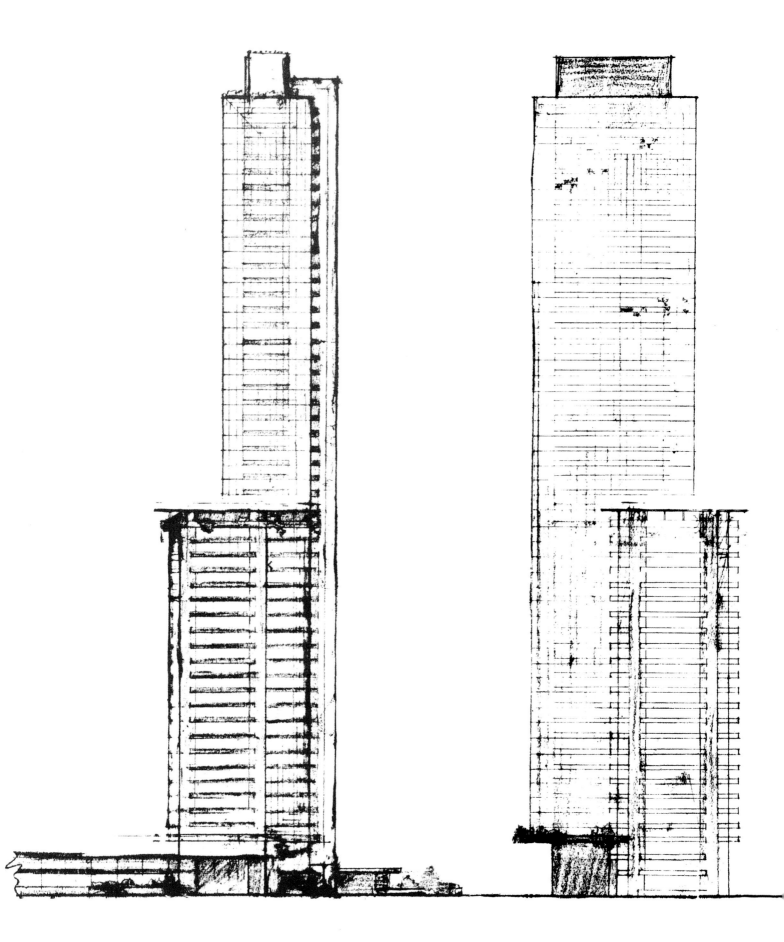

Sketches of front and side elevations
for skyscraper project, 1931

And it could stay thus, a feature of the Chicago lake front beautiful as the Eiffel Tower never was (and the Eiffel Tower would reach only well below its middle).

Something accomplished worthy of a century of progress? The beacons from the top would reach adjoining states: the radio from the antennae lifting from the tower crown, would be in touch with all the world.

But if not skyscraper-minded and preferring to roam instead of to be lifted up on high . . . then . . .

A weaving characteristic of this age of steel in tension. Accept from pioneer constructor John Roebling the message of the Brooklyn Bridge.

Build noble pylons—the Fair commissioners seemed to like the word pylon— on the Lake Front five hundred feet apart each way until enough park, including threading waterways, has been covered to accommodate all exhibitors on park level and one balcony. A canopy would be anchored by steel cables to the outer series of pylons. Weave main and minor and intermediate cables, a network to support transparent glass substitutes, and thus make an architectural canopy more beauti- ful and more vast than any ever seen. The canopy could rise five hundred feet at the pylons, to fall between them to one hundred and fifty feet above the park. The fabric should fall at the sides as a screen to close the space against wind. Rain would wash the roof spaces or they could be flushed from the pylon tops as foun- tains, the water spouting through openings at the low points of the canopy into fountain basins, features of the lagoons that would wind and thread their way beneath the canopy through the greenery of the park.

All trees, foliage and waterways could be joined by moving walkways reaching individual plots allotted to exhibitors. Little footwork for the beholders. Each indi- vidual exhibitor would be free to set up his own show and ballyhoo it as he pleased.

The old fair spirit, exciting as of old—but made free to excite the sophisticated modern ego once more by great spans and wondrous spinning.

Well, this type of construction with appropriate illumination and hydroelectric effects should cost less in standardization thus extended and made beautiful than the pettifogging, picture-making, individualized buildings of so many architects, all only interfering with exhibits and exhibitions in order to say exactly nothing in the same old way. Tagged—publicity tagged only—as new. At least, the great pylons might remain as lighting features of Lake Front Park; whereas the hodge- podge of buildings faked in synthetic cardboard and painted, would all have to be thrown away some day.

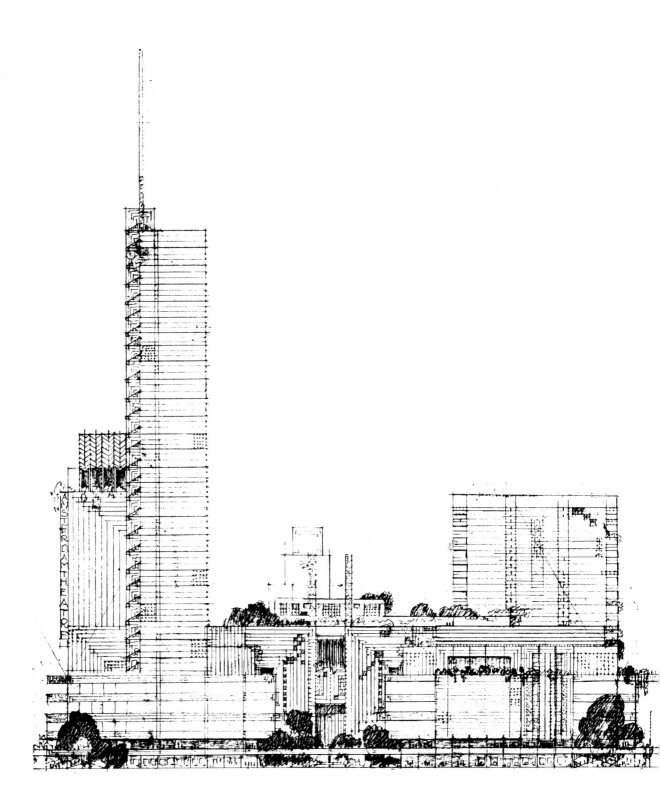

Sketch (1931) of skyscrapers properly related to streets,

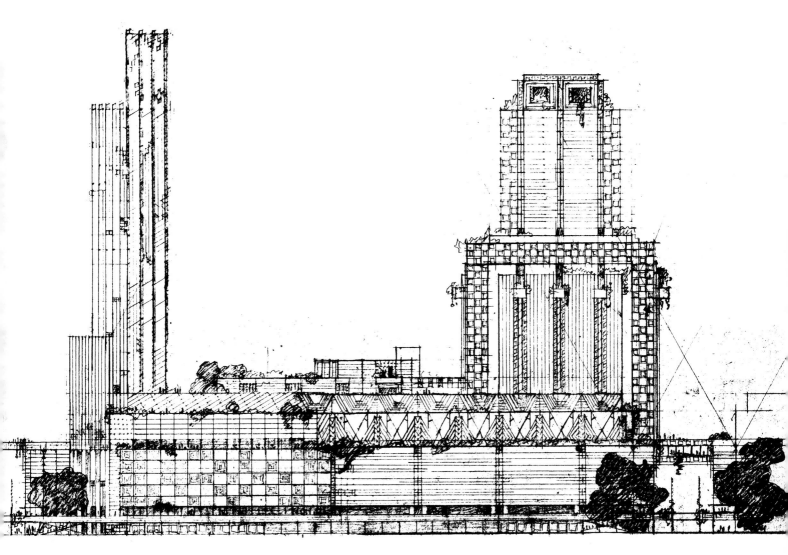

assuring light and air where needed, preventing congested traffic

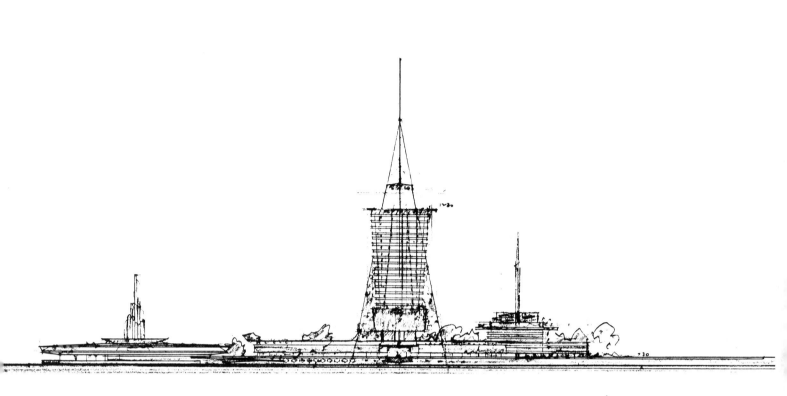

ELEVATION   LOOKING   NORTHEAST
SCALE   1" = 200'

Preliminary sketch for proposed
development of Point Park,
Pittsburgh, Pa., 1947

Or . . . more romantically inclined? Then why not—

There on the Lake Front is the Chicago harbor, already enclosed against the turbulence of Lake Michigan. Why not use that for a genuine holiday? A gay festival for the eye.

Why not a pontoon fair?

Make sealed, lightly reinforced metal cylinders, exhaust air from these like those of the catamaran; use them for floating foundations. Fabricate light thin tubes, some large, others not so large, some slender, and each in any desired length. Fabricate them in pulp to be very light, soaked and stiffened in waterproofing or in transparent synthetics. Use these "reeds" in rhythmic verticality, grouping them to get support for light roof-webbing. Again use the steel strand, anchored in metal drums, to get and hold the webbing for roof cover. Large pontoons for tall buildings, long buildings. Square for square buildings. All to be connected by interesting floating bridges. Floating gardens too could be connected to the buildings—the whole of the assembled floating units connected by characteristic link units, themselves attractive features, so that while all were joined, yet all might gently undulate with no harm.

Then introduce transparent colored glass tubing among the colored pulp tubing. Why not illuminate the glass and have, for once, airy verticality as a sheer legitimate modern fabrication, only aimed at as "a charm of New York" and there seen only at night in the rain?

The particolored opaque and transparent verticality would be doubled by direct reflections trembling in the water.

The water itself could again be thrown up to great heights and in enormous quantity by inserted force-pumps, effects costing nothing but power. Fair a whole world of illumination, irradiating and irradiated light—an iridescent fair or a fair of iridescent, opalescent "reeds."

The great whole would be a picturesque, pleasurable float.

Modern pageantry, this, and genuine in itself. Space could easily be created for specific purposes and adapted to suit each commercial need: these varied units linked together as a continuous, varied, brilliant modern circumstance.

Then, after the Fair was over, appropriate units could be detached and floated to an anchorage in the lagoons of the various parks and waterways of the Lake Front to serve as restaurants or good-time places, concessions rented from the city.

If there are these three ideas, genuine and practical as modern architecture, 1932a there could be as easily three hundred to choose from for the Fair.

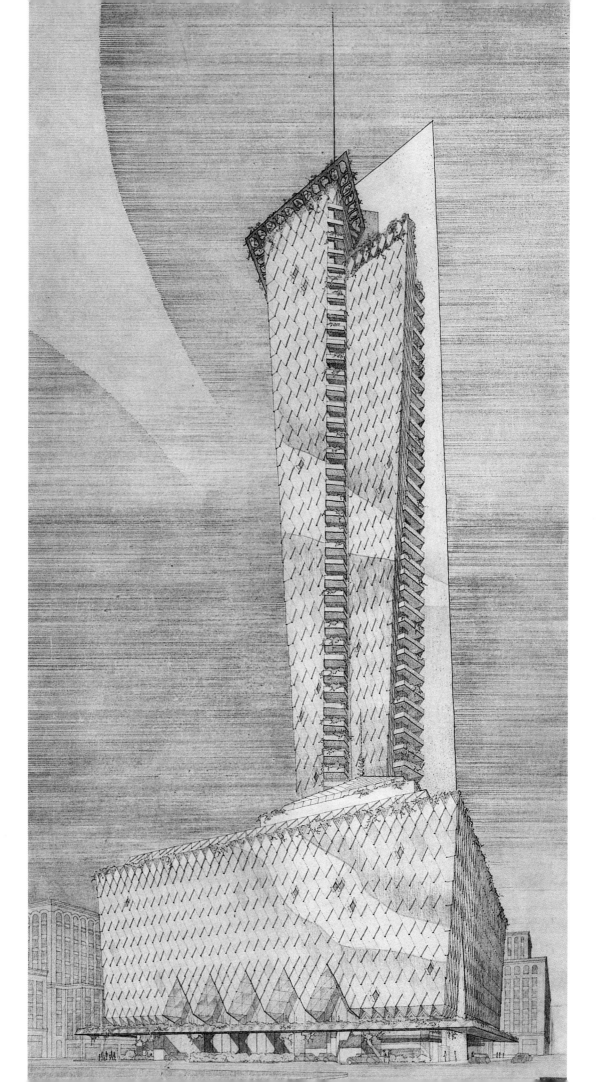

134

Glass walls hung from cantilevered floors; project for Roger Lacy Hotel, Dallas, Tex., 1947

SOME CASE HISTORIES

THE LARKIN BUILDING

Here, in the Larkin Building in Buffalo in 1904, was the first great assertion that the machine in the artist's hands is a great tool and will give works of art. But only if it is in the hands of the creative artist. The speech I made about the machine in 1901 at Hull House, pointing out the machine could be used for freedom, to emancipate the artist from the petty structural deceit of making things seem what they are not—well, Jane Addams wrote an editorial about that speech. It was printed in the *Architectural Record* in 1908 and reprinted in Europe.

1953a

It is interesting that I, an architect supposed to be concerned with the aesthetic sense of the building, should have invented the hung wall for the w.c. (easier to clean under), and adopted many other innovations like the glass door, steel furniture, air conditioning and radiant or "gravity heat." Nearly every technological innovation used today was suggested in the Larkin Building in 1904.

The Larkin Administration Building was a simple cliff of brick hermetically sealed (one of the first air-conditioned buildings in the country) to keep the interior space clear of the poisonous gases in the smoke from the . . . trains that puffed along beside it.

It was built of masonry materials—brick and stone; in terms of the straight line and flat plane the Larkin Administration Building was a genuine expression of power directly applied to purpose, in the same sense that the ocean liner, the plane or the car is so. And it's only fair to say that it has had a profound influence upon European architecture for this reason.

And I worked to get that principle of articulation into the Larkin Building. But not until the contract had been let to Paul Mueller and the plaster model of the building stood completed on the big detail board at the center of the Oak Park drafting room did I get the articulation I finally wanted. The solution that had hung fire came in a flash. I took the next train to Buffalo to try and get the Larkin Company to see that it was worth thirty thousand dollars more to build the stair towers free of the central block, not only as independent stair towers for communication and escape but also as air intakes for the ventilating system. It would require this sum to individualize and properly articulate these features as I saw them.

Mr. Larkin, a kind and generous man, granted the appropriation and the building as architecture, I felt, was saved.

This entire building was a great fireproof vault, probably the first completely fireproof furnished building. The furniture was all made in steel and magnesite built into place—even the desks and chairs we made with the building. I never had a chance to design the telephone or the wastepaper baskets I had in mind as the office had already arranged for both these items. All else was of or with the building.

Magnesite was a new material to us then, but it was probably the cement used by the Romans and good in Rome until today. We experimented with it—finally used it—throughout the interior. And I made many new inventions. The hanging water-closet partition, the long, automatic multiple-chair desk, were among them. All were intended to simplify cleaning and make operation easy. The dignified, top-lighted interior created the effect of one great official family at work in clean and airy quarters, day-lit and officered from a central court. The top story was a restaurant and conservatory, the ferns and flowers seen from the court below. The roof was a recreation ground paved with brick. The new architecture was in every detail practical. . . .

1932a

An exhibition at the Art Institute of Chicago showing steel office furniture designed for and used in the Larkin Company building, 1904

Below, balcony office; right, central court: Larkin
Company building, Buffalo, N. Y., 1904

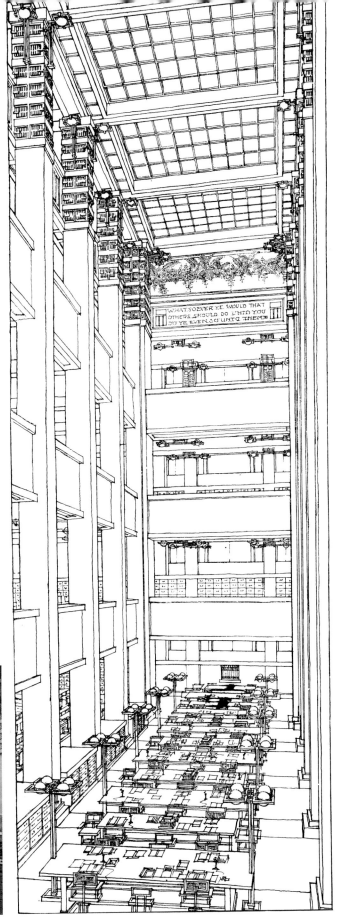

Unity Church and community house, Oak Park, Ill., 1906

UNITY TEMPLE

The Unity Temple of 1906 was reinforced concrete. It was the first building to come complete as architecture cast from forms. The idea of the reality of the building as the space within had found tangible expression. I was quite pleased with myself in the Unity Temple. I thought I was prophetic and had made a statement bound to re-create the world of architecture.

Its significance was, emphasis on what is called the third dimension. It is not thickness, but depth, a sense of space. All this added up to a new dispensation as to what might constitute the life of a building: it could parallel the life of the free individual.

1953a

The first idea was to keep a noble room for worship in mind, and let that sense of the great room shape the whole edifice. Let the room inside be the architecture outside.

What shape? Well, the answer lay in the material. There was only one material to choose—as the church funds were $45,000—to "church" four hundred people in 1906. Concrete was cheap.

Why not make the wooden boxes or forms so the concrete could be cast in them as separate blocks and masses, these grouped about an interior space in some such way as to preserve this sense of the interior space, the great room, in the appearance of the whole building? And the block-masses might be left as themselves with no facing at all? That would be cheap and permanent and not ugly either.

What roof? What had concrete to offer as a cover shelter? The concrete slab—of course. The reinforced slab. Nothing else if the building was to be thorough-bred, meaning built-in character out of one material.

Too monumental, all this? Too forthright for my committee I feared. Would a statement so positive as that final slab over the whole seem irreligious to them? Profane in their eyes? Why? But the flat slab was cheap and direct. It would be nobly simple. The wooden forms or molds in which concrete buildings must at

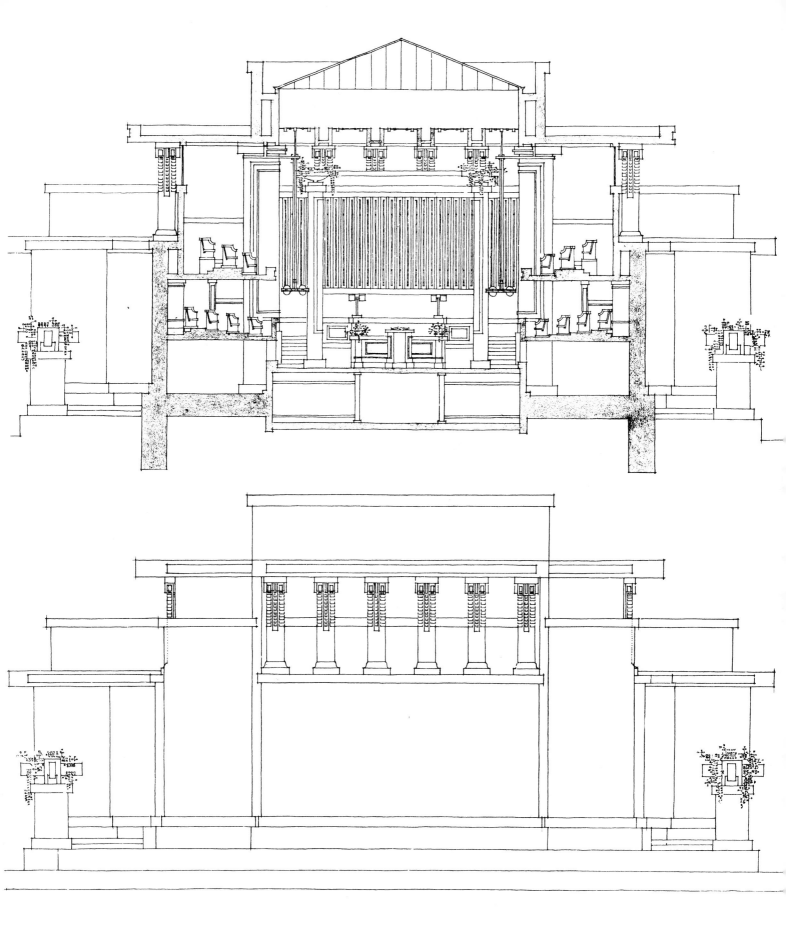

"That sense of the great room"
Above, section through building; below, elevation: Unity Church, Oak Park, Ill., 1906

141

that time be cast were always the chief item of expense, so to repeat the use of a single form as often as possible was necessary. Therefore a building, all four sides alike, looked like the thing. This, reduced to simplest terms, meant a building square in plan. That would make their temple a cube—a noble form in masonry.

The slab, too, belonged to the cube by nature. "Credo simplicitatem." That form is most imaginative and happy that is most radiant with the aura or overtone of super-form. Integrity.

Then the temple itself—still in my mind—began to take shape. The site was noisy, by the Lake Street car tracks. Therefore it seemed best to keep the building closed on the three street sides and enter it from a court to the rear at the center of the lot. Unity Temple itself, with the thoughts in mind I have just expressed, arrived easily enough but there was a secular side to Unitarian church activities —entertainment often, Sunday school, feasts, and so on.

To embody these with the temple would spoil the simplicity of the room—the noble room in the service of man for the worship of God. So I finally put the secular space designated as Unity House to the rear of the lot, as a long building to be subdivided by movable screens for Sunday school or other occasions. It thus became a separate building but harmonious with the temple—the entrance to both to be the connecting link between them. That was that.

And why not put the pulpit at the entrance side, at the rear of the square Temple and bring the congregation into the room at the sides, on a lower level, so those entering would be imperceptible to the audience? This would preserve the quiet and the dignity of the room itself. Out of that thought came the depressed foyer or cloister corridor on either side, leading from the main lobby at the center to the stairs in the near and far corners of the room. Those entering the room in this way could see into the big room but not be seen by those already seated within it.

And, important to the pastor, when the congregation rose to disperse, here was their opportunity to move forward toward their pastor. Wide doors beside the pulpit allowed the entire flock to pass out by him and find themselves directly in the entrance loggia from which they had first come in.

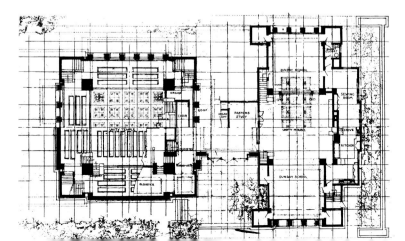

Plan of Unity Church and community house, Oak Park, Ill., 1906

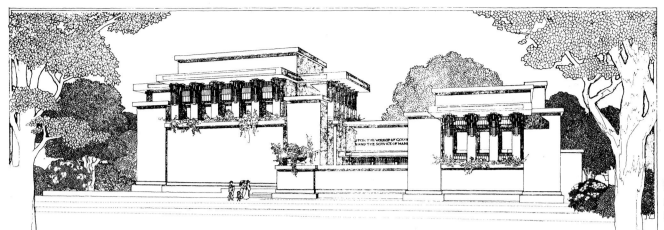

Unity Church and community house, Oak Park, Ill., 1906

So this was done.

The room itself—size determined by comfortable seats with leg-room for four hundred people—was built with four interior free-standing posts to carry the overhead structure. These concrete posts were hollow and became ducts to insure economic and uniform distribution of heat. The large supporting posts were so set as to form alcoves on four sides of the room. I flooded these side alcoves with light from above to get a sense of a happy cloudless day into the room. And with this feeling for light, the center ceiling between the four great posts became skylight; daylight sifting through between the intersecting concrete beams, filtering through amber glass ceiling lights. Thus managed, the light would, rain or shine, have the warmth of sunlight. Artificial lighting shone from the same place there at night as well. This scheme of lighting was integral, gave diffusion and kept the room clear.

But return to the drawing board; here we see penciled upon a sheet of paper, the plan, section, and elevation in the main—all except the exterior of Unity House, as the room for secular recreation is to be called. To establish harmony between these buildings of separate function proved difficult, utterly exasperating.

Another series of concentrations—lasting hours at a time for several days. How to keep the noble scale of the temple in the design of the subordinate mass of the secular hall and not falsify the function of that secular mass? The ideal of an organic architecture is often terribly severe discipline for the imagination. I came to know that full well. And, always, some minor concordance takes more time, taxes concentration more than all besides. Any minor element may become a major problem to vex the architect. How many schemes I have thrown away because some one minor feature would not come true to form!

Thirty-four studies were necessary to arrive at this concordance as it is now seen. Unfortunately the studies are lost with thousands of others of many other buildings: the fruit of similar struggles to coordinate and perfect them as organic entities—I wish I had kept them. Unity House looks easy enough now, for it is right enough. But it was not.

Finally, see the sense of the room not only preserved—it may be seen as the soul of the design. Instead of being carved from the heart of a block of building material, hid from sight, the sacrosanct space for worship is merely screened in ... does it come through as the living motif of the architecture?

Many studies in detail as a matter of course yet remain to be made to determine what further may be left out to protect the design. These studies never seem to end and in this sense no organic building may ever be finished. The complete goal of the ideal of organic architecture is never reached. Nor need be. What worth-while ideal is ever reached?

Unity Temple is a complete building on paper, already. There is no sketch and there never has been one. There seldom is in a thought-built building.

1932a

TALIESIN

Finally it was not so easy to tell where pavements and walls left off and ground began. Especially on the hill-crown, which became a low-walled garden above the surrounding courts, reached by stone steps walled into the slopes. A clump of fine oaks that grew on the hilltop stood untouched on one side above the court. A great curved stone-walled seat enclosed the space just beneath them, and stone pavement stepped down to a spring or fountain that welled up into a pool at the center of the circle. Each court had its fountain and the winding stream below had a great dam. A thick stone wall was thrown across it, to make a pond at the very foot of the hill and raise the water in the valley to within sight from

Taliesin. The water below the falls thus made was sent by hydraulic ram up to a big stone reservoir built into a higher hill, just behind and above the hilltop garden, to come down again into the fountains and again down to the vegetable gardens on the slopes below the house.

The finished wood outside was the color of gray tree trunks in violet light.

The shingles of the roof surfaces were left to weather silver-gray like the tree branches spreading below them.

Chimneys of the great stone fireplaces rose heavily through all, wherever there was a gathering place within, and there were many such places. Great rock slabs bridged over deep hearth openings inside; outside were strong, quiet rectangular rock masses bespeaking strength and comfort within.

Above, exterior of master bedroom; below, a fireplace: Taliesin, Spring Green, Wis., 1925

Left, hilltop wing, Taliesin, Spring Green, Wis., 1925

Country masons laid all the stone, with the stone quarry for a pattern and the architect for a teacher. The masons learned to lay the walls in the long, thin, flat ledges natural to the quarry, natural edges out. As often as they laid a stone they would stand back to judge the effect. They were soon as interested as sculptors fashioning a statue; one might imagine they were, as they stepped back, head cocked one side, to get the general effect. Having arrived at some conclusion they would step forward and shove the stone more to their liking, seeming never to tire of this discrimination. Many of them were artistic for the first time, and liked it.

Screened porch of loggia, guest room below: Taliesin

The workmen took the work as a sort of adventure. It was adventure. In every realm. Especially in the financial realm. I kept working all the while to make the money come. It did. And we kept on inside with plenty of clean soft wood that could be left alone pretty much in plain surfaces. The stone, too, strong and protective inside, spoke for itself in certain piers and walls.

Inside floors, like the outside floors, were stone paved or if not were laid with wide, dark-streaked cypress boards. The plaster in the walls was mixed with raw sienna in the box, went onto the walls natural, drying out tawny gold. Outside, the plastered walls were the same but grayer with cement. But in the constitution of the whole, in the way the walls rose from the plan, and spaces were roofed over, was the chief interest of the house. The whole was supremely natural. The rooms went up into the roof, tentlike, and were ribanded overhead with marking-strips

Covered terrace, Taliesin, Spring Green, Wis., 1925

Terrace of master bedroom, Taliesin, Spring Green, Wis., 1925

of waxed soft wood. The house was set so sun came through the openings into every room sometime during the day. Walls opened everywhere to views as the windows swung out above the tree-tops, tops of red, white and black oaks and wild cherry trees festooned with wild grapevines. In spring, the perfume of the blossoms came full through the windows, the birds singing there the while, from 1932a sunrise to sunset—all but the several white months of winter.

House and land, Taliesin, Spring Green, Wis., 1925

THE IMPERIAL HOTEL

Detail, Imperial Hotel,
Tokyo, Japan, 1915-22

Now in 1914 came an expedition from Japan looking for an architect to build their new Imperial Hotel. They came around the world by way of Europe and on their way to America they heard my name and knew the German publication of my work. They heard the name again and again in Europe and decided to look me up. They saw the buildings and said, "Well, not Japanese, not at all, but will look well in Japan."

Thereupon, I spent six years on studies of earthquake conditions. It never left my consciousness. And we solved the problem of the menace of the quake by concluding that rigidity couldn't be the answer, and that flexibility and resiliency must be the answer. So we built this building. It could flex and return to normal. And it did withstand the great quakes.

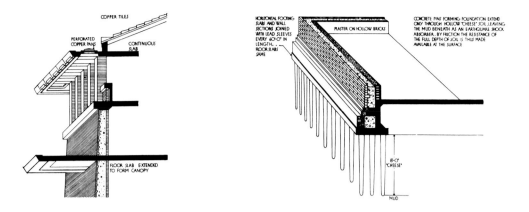

Construction details, Imperial Hotel

But also, for the first time in the history of Japan a foreigner had taken off his hat to her culture and tried to build with Western technology without losing what was precious and beautiful in her own culture. The Imperial Hotel had not only to withstand the earthquake but also to be worthy to stand without annoyance and insolence in Japan.

1953a

I studied the temblor. Found it a wave-movement, not of sea but of earth—accompanied by terrific shocks no rigidity could withstand.

Because of the wave movements, deep foundations like long piles would oscillate and rock the structure. Therefore the foundation should be short or shallow. There was sixty to seventy feet of soft mud below eight feet of surface soil on the site. That mud seemed a merciful provision—a good cushion to relieve the terrible shocks. Why not float the building upon it?—a battleship floats on salt water. And why not extreme lightness combined with tenuity and flexibility instead of the great weight required by the greatest possible rigidity? Why not, then, a building made as the two hands thrust together palms inward, fingers inter-locking and yielding to movement—but resilient to return to original position when distortion ceased? A flexure—flexing and reflexing in any direction. Why fight the quake? Why not sympathize with it and outwit it?

That was how the building began to be planned.

The most serious problem was how to get the most carrying power out of that eight feet of cheeselike soil that overlay the liquid mud. During the first year of plan making, I made borings nine inches in diameter eight feet deep and filled them with concrete. Arranged to test the concrete pins thus made. Got carloads

Work in progress, Imperial Hotel. From left to right: pile driving; concrete pins spaced two feet from center to center; lava to be carved as trim: photo taken March 26, 1921

150

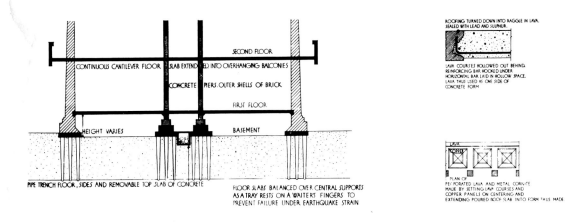

ROOFING TURNED DOWN INTO RAGGLE IN LAVA. SEALED WITH LEAD AND SULPHUR.

LAVA COURSES HOLLOWED OUT BEHIND. REINFORCING BAR HOOKED UNDER HORIZONTAL BAR LAID IN HOLLOW SPACE. LAVA THUS USED AS ONE SIDE OF CONCRETE FORM

SECOND FLOOR

CONTINUOUS CANTILEVER FLOOR SLAB EXTENDED INTO OVERHANGING BALCONIES

CONCRETE PIERS OUTER SHELLS OF BRICK

FIRST FLOOR

HEIGHT VARIES   BASEMENT

PIPE TRENCH FLOOR, SIDES AND REMOVABLE TOP SLAB OF CONCRETE

FLOOR SLABS BALANCED OVER CENTRAL SUPPORTS AS A TRAY RESTS ON A WAITER'S FINGERS TO PREVENT FAILURE UNDER EARTHQUAKE STRAIN

LAVA

PLAN OF PERFORATED LAVA AND METAL CORNICE MADE BY SETTING LAVA COURSES AND COPPER PANELS ON CENTERING AND EXTENDING POURED ROOF SLAB INTO FORM THUS MADE

of pig iron and loaded the pins until they would drive into the ground. Kept the test figures of loads and reactions. Took borings all over the site to find soft pockets. Water stood in the holes two feet below the surface, so the concrete had to go in as quickly as the borings were completed. Later, tapered piles were driven in to punch the holes and pulled out—the concrete thrown directly in as the pile was out of the way.

These data in hand, the foundation plan was made to push these concrete pins two feet on centers each way over the entire areas on which the wall footings were to spread. The strength of the whole depth of eight feet of topsoil was thus brought to bear at the surface. That was simple. But here was a compressible soil that might take a squeeze under the broad footings to add to the friction against the pins. Experiments showed the squeeze could safely be added to the friction. This meant a settlement of the building of five inches, the building itself driving the piles that much deeper. This was economy, but dangerous and more complicated.

But finally the building was computed pound by pound and distributed according to test data to float below the grade of the ground surface—and it did. With some few slight variations it stayed there.

This foundation saved hundreds of thousands of dollars over the foundations then in use in Tokyo. But had the owners of the Imperial known what was contemplated something might have happened to prevent it. Rumor nearly did prevent it. Here, however, was the desired shock absorber, a cushion, pins and all, ready to be uniformly loaded and put to work against the day of reckoning.

Now how to make a flexible structure instead of a foolish rigid one? Divide

the building into parts. Where the parts were necessarily more than sixty feet long, joint these parts, clear through floors, walls, footings and all, and manage the joints in the design. Wherever part met part, through joints also. So far, good sense, and careful calculation.

But a construction was needed where floors would not be carried between walls, because subterranean disturbances might move the walls and drop the floors. Why not then carry the floors as a waiter carries his tray on upraised arm and fingers at the center—balancing the load? All supports centered under the floor slabs like that instead of resting the slabs on the walls at their edges as is usually the case?

This meant the cantilever, as I had found by now. The cantilever is most romantic, most free, of all principles of construction, and in this case it seemed the most sensible. The waiter's tray supported by his hand at the center is a cantilever slab in principle. And so concrete cantilever slabs continuous across the building from side to side, supported in that way, became the structure of the Imperial Hotel at Tokyo.

Roof tiles of Japanese buildings have murdered countless thousands of Japanese in upheavals, so a light hand-worked green copper roof was planned. Why kill more?

The outer walls were spread wide, thick and heavy at the base, growing thinner and lighter toward the top. Whereas Tokyo buildings were all top-heavy, the center of gravity was kept low against the swinging quake movements and the wall slopes were made an aesthetic feature of the design. The outside ends of the cantilever slabs where they came through the walls were all lightened by ornamental perforations enriching the light and shade of the structure. The stone everywhere underfoot in Tokyo was a workable light lava weighing as much as green oak. It was considered sacrilege to use this common material for the aristocratic edifice. But finally it was used for the feature material and readily yielded to any sense of form the architect might choose to indicate. And the whole structure was set up as a double shell—an exterior of slim cunning bricks, and an interior of fluted hollow bricks raised together to a convenient height of four feet or more at a time. These shells were poured solid with concrete to bind them together.

Above, terrace; center, pool being filled;
below, courtyard during military occupation:
Imperial Hotel, Tokyo, Japan, 1915-22

The great building thus became a jointed monolith with a mosaic surface of lava and brick. Earthquakes had always torn piping and wiring apart where laid in the structure and had flooded or charged the building. So all piping and wiring was laid free of construction in covered concrete trenches in the basements, independent even of foundations. Mains and all pipes were of lead with wiped joints, the lead bends sweeping from the trenches to be hung free in vertical pipe shafts, from which the curved lead branches were again taken off, curved, to the stacks of bathrooms. Thus any disturbance might flex and rattle but not break the pipes or wiring.

Last but not least there was an immense reservoir or pool as an architectural feature of the entrance court—connected to the water system of the hotel and conserving the roof water.

Thus the plans were made so that all architectural features were practical necessities, and the straight line and flat plane were respectfully modified in point of style to a building bowing to the traditions of the people to whom the building would belong.

1932a

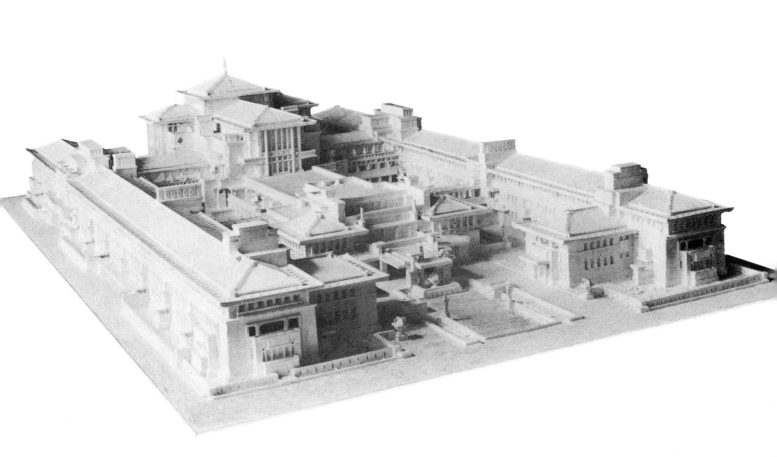

Plaster model (lost in transit to the U. S.) of Imperial Hotel, Tokyo, Japan, 1915-22

Entrance, Imperial Hotel, Tokyo, Japan, 1915-22

Above: lobby, brick and carved lava; right above: pierced brickwork, bronze urn, patterned carpeting; right below: porte-cochère, copper roofs, carved lava, pierced brick: Imperial Hotel, Tokyo, Japan, 1915-22

Canvas diffuses desert sun at Ocatillo, Arizona desert camp, 1927

OCATILLO

The box-board cabins are connected by a low box-board wall with a horizontal zigzag—for the same reason Thomas Jefferson worm-walled his brick. It will be self-supporting and this will complete the compound. Necessary openings in the canvas-topped box buildings we will close with canvas-covered wood frames. Flaps hinged with rubber belting. No glazed doors or windows. Glass is not for this type of desert camp if indeed glass belongs in the desert at all.

Now, when all these white canvas wings, like sails, are spread, the buildings will look something like ships coming down the mesa, rigged like ships balanced in the breeze.

Cabins, and experimental blocks for San Marcos hotel project, at Ocatillo, Arizona desert camp, 1927

Yes, the group will look like some new kind of desert fleet. We painted the horizontal boards with cold-water paint, continuing around the varied board wall connecting all the cabins about the mound. I chose dry rose as the color to match the light on the desert floor. The one-two triangle we used in planning the camp is made by the mountain ranges around about the site. And the one-two triangle is the cross section of the talus at their bases. This triangle is reflected in the general forms of all the cabins as well as the general plan. We will paint the canvas triangles in the eccentric gables, scarlet. This red triangular form in the treatment is why we called the camp Ocatillo. Candle flame.

I presently found that the white luminous canvas overhead and canvas used instead of window glass afforded such agreeable diffusion of light within, was so enjoyable and sympathetic to the desert, that I now felt more than ever oppressed by the thought of the opaque solid overhead of the much too heavy midwestern house.

The desert devils would come whirling like a dancing dervish and go in drifting spirals of dust rising high in the air. Occasionally a devil would cross the camp and it would shudder in its grasp like a ship—but hold fast. No damage.

I believe we pay too slight attention to making slight buildings beautiful or beautiful buildings slight. Lightness and strength may now be synonymous.

Usually we spend so much too much to make buildings last as we say. Unqualified to build, we are still busy making caves for survivals.

So, Ocatillo—our little desert camp—you are an ephemera.

The little camp is finished. We love it. The canvas windows of Ocatillo are like ship sails when open and may shut against dust or may open part way to deflect the desert breezes into the interiors. Screened openings for cross ventilation are everywhere at the floor levels, a discovery I made in seeking coolness, to be used during the heat of the day; closed at night. The long sides of the canvas slopes lie easily with the lines of the landscape stretching themselves wide open toward the sun in order to aid a little in warming the interiors in winter. This long canvas roof-side is to have additional cover of canvas, air blowing between the two sheets, if the camp is ever occupied in summer. We can add this later if we stay on in summer, and make it belong.

Finally to justify our wild adventure, Ocatillo cost not so much more than the rent and keep asked for equivalent accommodations in Chandler or in Phoenix for the one season we were to stay. The cost was about two hundred dollars per cabin. The labor was mostly our own. We are the better for that labor. We have met the desert, loved it and lived with it, and the desert is ours.

1932a

The compound at Ocatillo, Arizona desert camp, 1927

Hotel, planned for San-Marcos-in-the-Desert near Chandler, Ariz., 1927

SAN MARCOS

We worked out the resort as a great block-system, a series of intercommunicating terraces facing to the sun of the south. There were three terraces, one rising above the other against the mountainside, each room on them having its own pool and garden. The block system started in La Miniatura in this case was genuine reinforced masonry, the same within and without. The shell became the structure itself.

The deep wash or ravine rising between two great hills back of the terraces, we used to conceal the road leading to the main entrance of the building. This entrance was placed well back under the building in the gorge itself. An organ tower of copper and concrete block rose like a giant sahuaro here to emphasize this entrance, intended to give voice to the whole. Echo-organs were planned in the hills—Dr. Chandler's idea—for open-air vesper concerts in the desert.

The dining room? Simply a top-lit glass and copper arbor above the central living room mass and so connected to the hill slopes on either side by the upper terraces of the wings that adjacent dwellers in the mountain cottages—to be built later on as a part of the whole—could reach it comfortably on foot along this level.

The plan of this far-flung, long-drawn-out building, owing to the levels of the sunlit terraces, was such that each room, each bathroom, each closet, each corridor even, had direct sunlight. Every portion of the building to be lived in was free to the sun and also to magnificent views. The whole building had the warm southern exposure every winter resort covets. And, the whole structure approximated what we call permanence, say three hundred years at least. Three hundred large rooms with bath, all appurtenance systems more than adequate and virtually indestructible too.

Now, observe if you will that every horizontal line in San Marcos in the Desert was a dotted line. Every flat plane was grosgrained like the sahuaro itself. The entire building, in pattern, was an abstraction of mountain region and cactus life, set up in permanent masonry shells. But none the less, rather more a human habitation to live in as long maybe as the mountain lasts.

1932a

THE JOHNSON ADMINISTRATION BUILDING

The building was laid out upon a horizontal-unit system, twenty feet on centers both ways; it rose into the air on a vertical-unit system of 3½ inches: one especially

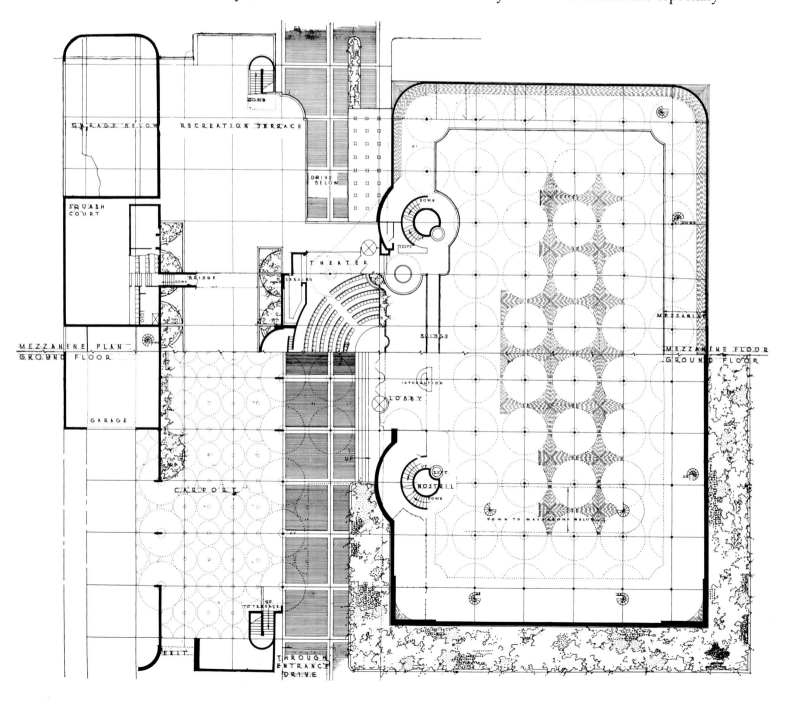

large brick course. Glass was not used as brick in this structure; bricks were bricks. The building itself became crystal by way of long glass tubing where either transparence or translucence was felt to be appropriate. To make the structure monolithic the enclosing wall-material appeared inside wherever it was sensible to do so.

The main feature of construction was the simple repetition of slender, hollow, monolithic dendriform shafts ending in small brass shoes embedded at floor level

Left, interior under construction; right, hollow column subjected to test loads: S. C. Johnson and Son administration building, Racine, Wis., 1936

By way of a natural use of steel in tension, weight in this building appears to lift and float in light and air; miraculous light dendriforms standing up against the sky take on integral character, plastic units of a plastic building construction, emphasizing space instead of standing in the way as mere inserts for support.

The great structure throughout is light and plastic; an open glass-filled rift is up there where the cornice might have been.

The entire steel-reinforced structure stands there earthquake-proof, fireproof,

Plan, S. C. Johnson and Son administration building, Racine, Wis., 1936 soundproof, and vermin-proof. Reinforcing was mostly cold-drawn steel mesh —welded.

The main clerical work force was all correlated in one vast air-conditioned room, 228 by 228 feet. This great room, besides top lighting and the rift for light at cornice level, is daylit also by rifts in the brick walls. The heating system of the main building is entirely beneath the floor slab; the structure is hermetically sealed and air-conditioned, with gravity heat.

The building, destined to stand in unimpressive surroundings bounded by three ordinary village streets, has the main entrance interior to the building lot; thus the modern indispensable motor car was provided for, and with new hospitality. Ample parking facilities are under the cover of a great domiculated carport.

The main building itself in which the dendriform shafts float, is set back from the street on three sides; a colorful band of planting divides brick walls from sidewalks, enlivening the environment. The carport roof, tile-paved, was to become a playground for the workers.

A cinema seating 250 for lectures or entertainment, wired complete for sound, is placed at mezzanine level. A glass-enclosed bridge connects executive offices in the penthouse to a tall wood-lined squash court rising high above the garage.

Below this penthouse opens a view of the big workroom on the ground level, with the several hundred office workers sitting at especially devised desks on chairs that belong with the desks. Subheads of various departments function just above in a low mezzanine to the big room where direct vision and prompt connection with the workers is had by spiral iron stairways at convenient points.

The few enclosures within the big workroom have low glass walls, screened by Aero-shades. Thus the stimulating sense of the whole is well preserved even to the uttermost detail.

1943a

Detail showing construction and furnishing,
S. C. Johnson and Son administration building

Interior,
S. C. Johnson and Son
administration building,
Racine, Wis., 1936

WINGSPREAD

This structure is of the common prairie type of earlier years; a type proving itself good for a home in the climate around the Great Lakes. The construction is popularly known as brick veneer. Upper surfaces are wide cypress plank, roofs are tiled, floors, concrete with four-foot-square tiles over floor heating, here as in the Administration Building itself.

Thus Wingspread, unique prairie house near Racine, became another in the series of zoning experiments beginning with the Coonley House at Riverside, built

Plan of Wingspread, Wind Point, Wis., 1937

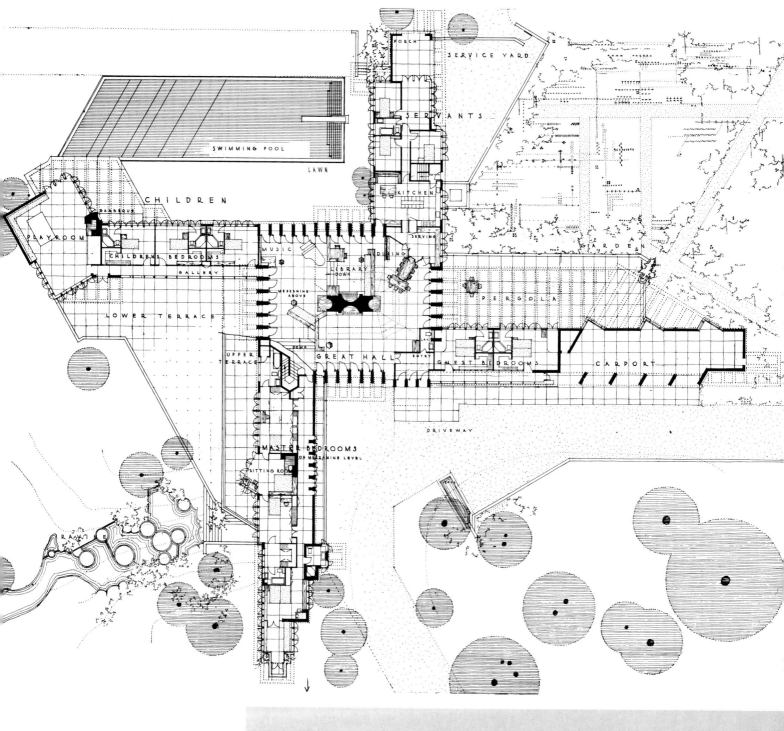

SWIMMING POOL

LAWN

CHILDREN

PORCH

SERVICE YARD

SERVANTS

KITCHEN

GARDEN

BARBEQUE

PLAYROOM

CHILDRENS BEDROOMS

GALLERY

MUSIC

SERVING

DINING

LIBRARY
DOWN

MEZZANINE ABOVE

PERGOLA

LOWER TERRACE

UPPER TERRACE

DOWN

GREAT HALL

ENTRY

GUEST BEDROOMS

CARPORT

DRIVEWAY

MASTER BEDROOMS
ON MEZZANINE LEVEL

SITTING ROOM

1909, where living room, dining room, kitchen, family sleeping rooms, guest rooms, were separate units grouped together and connected by corridors.

The building is orientated so that sunlight falls in all rooms and the ground plan shows a complete logical expression of a zoned house.

At the center of four zones forming a cross, stands a spacious wigwam of a living room. A tall central brick chimney stack with five fireplaces on four sides divides this large vertical central living space into four areas for the various domestic functions: entrance, family living, library, and dining room. Extending from this great, dignified central wigwam are the four wings. This extended plan lies, very much at home, quiet and integral with the prairie landscape which is, through it, made more significant and beautiful. In this case, especially, green growth will eventually claim its own; wild grapevines pendent from the generously spreading trellises, extensive gardens in bloom, extending beneath them, great masses of evergreens on two sides and one taller, dense, dark-green mass set on a low mound in the middle of the entrance court—the single tall associate of this spreading wigwam on the prairie. Lake Michigan lies well off ahead but within the middle distance, and is seen over the wildfowl pool which stretches away just below the main terrace of the house, a charming foreground.

This house, while resembling the Coonley House at Riverside, Illinois, is more bold, masculine, and direct in form and treatment. It is better executed, in more permanent materials. The building has a heavy footing course of Kasota sandstone resting on rock ballast laid deep in broad trenches, has the best brickwork I have seen in my life, and the materials of construction and the workmanship throughout are everywhere substantial. Especially the woodwork and furniture show fine craftsmanship. The house is architecturally furnished throughout in good keeping with the quiet character established by the building.

1943a

Wingspread, Wind Point, Wis., 1937

THE SMALL HOUSE

Clients have asked me: "How far should we go out, Mr. Wright?" I say: "Just ten times as far as you think you ought to go." So my suggestion would be to go just as far as you can go—and go soon and fast.

There is only one solution, one principle, one proceeding which can rid the city of its congestion—decentralization. . . . The only answer to life today is to get back to the good ground, or rather I should say, to get forward to it, because now instead of going back, we can go forward to the ground: not the city going to the country but the country and city becoming one. We have the means to go, a means that is entirely adequate to human purposes where life is now most concerned. Because we have the automobile, we can go far and fast and when we get there, we have other machines to use—the tractor or whatever else you may want to use.

We have all the means to live free and independent, far apart—as we choose— still retaining all the social relationships and advantages we ever had, even to have them greatly multiplied. No matter if we do have houses a quarter of a mile apart. You would enjoy all that you used to enjoy when you were ten to a block, and think of the immense advantages for your children and for yourself: freedom to use the ground, relationship with all kinds of living growth.

With a small budget the best kind of land to build on is flat land. Of course, if you can get a gentle slope, the building will be more interesting, more satisfactory. But changes of ground surface make building much more expensive.

One of the best foundations I know, suitable to many places (particularly to frost regions), was devised by the old Welsh stonemason who put in the foundations for buildings now used by Taliesin North. Instead of digging down three and a half feet or four feet below the frost line, as was standard practice in Wisconsin, not only terribly expensive but rendering capillary attraction a threat to the upper wall, he dug shallow trenches about sixteen inches deep and slightly pitched them to a drain. These trenches he filled with broken stone about the size of your fist. Broken stone does not clog up, and provides the drainage beneath the wall that saves it from being lifted by the frost.

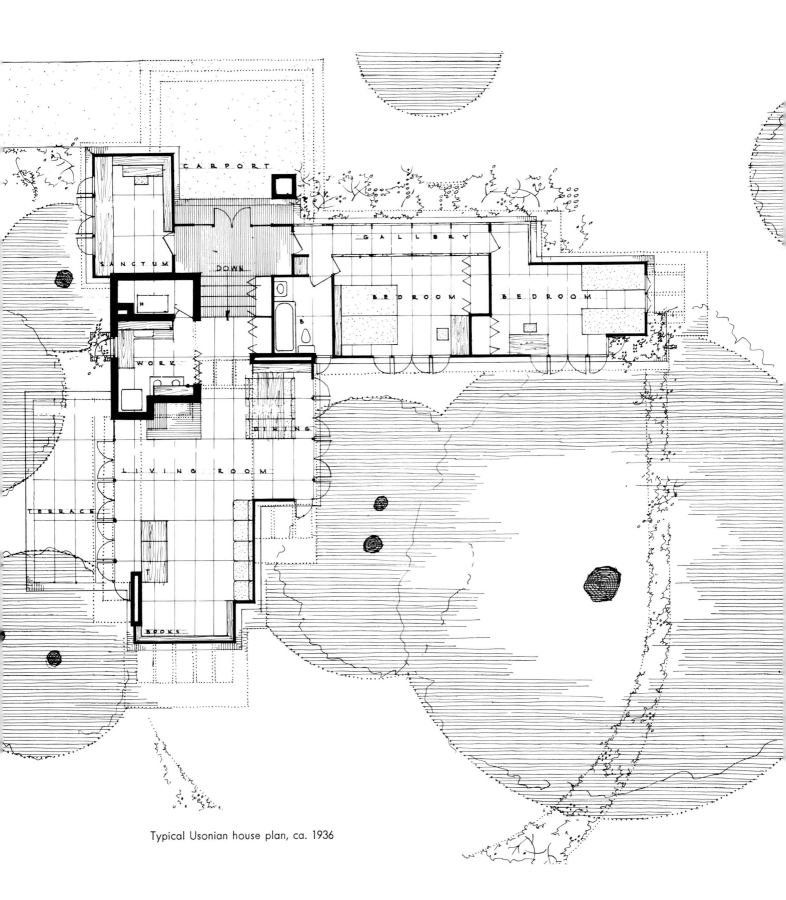

CARPORT

GALLERY

SANCTUM

DOWN

BEDROOM

BEDROOM

WORK

B

DINING

LIVING ROOM

TERRACE

BOOKS

Typical Usonian house plan, ca. 1936

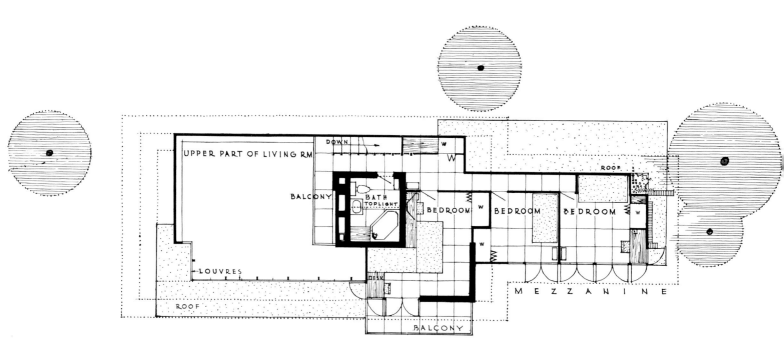

UPPER PART OF LIVING RM

DOWN

BALCONY

BATH
TOPLIGHT

BEDROOM   BEDROOM   BEDROOM

ROOF

LOUVRES

ROOF

DESK

MEZZANINE

BALCONY

Above, upper level; below, ground
floor: plans of two-story Usonian house
for the Ellinwoods, Deerfield, Ill., 1941

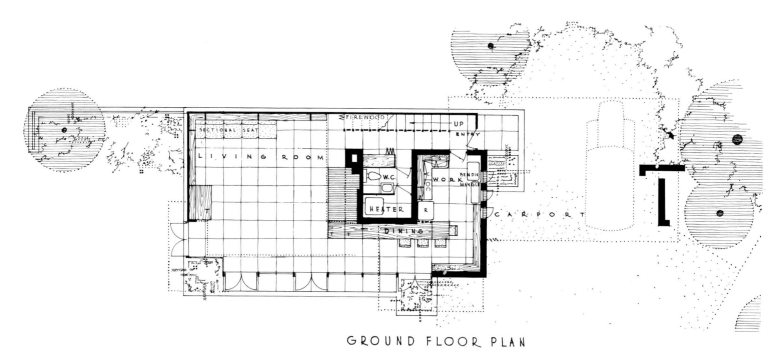

SECTIONAL SEAT

LIVING ROOM

FIREWOOD

UP

ENTRY

W.C.

WORK

BENDIX
MANGLE

HEATER

R

DINING

CARPORT

GROUND FLOOR PLAN

I have called it the dry-wall footing, because if the wall stayed dry the frost could not affect it. In a region of deep cold to keep a building from moving it is necessary to get all water (or moisture) from underneath it. If there is no water there to freeze, the foundation cannot be lifted. (That type of footing, however, is not applicable to treacherous subsoils, where the problem is entirely different.)

1954a

... It is necessary to use work in the mill to good advantage, necessary to eliminate, so far as possible, field labor which is always expensive: it is necessary to consolidate and simplify the three appurtenance systems—heating, lighting, and sanitation. At least this must be our economy if we are to achieve the sense of spaciousness and vista we desire in order to liberate the people living in the house. And it would be ideal to complete the building in one operation as it goes along. Inside and outside should be complete in one operation. The house finished inside as it is completed outside. There should be no complicated roofs.

To assist in general planning, what must or may we use in our new construction? In this case five materials: wood, brick, cement, paper, glass. To simplify fabrication we must use our horizontal-unit system in construction. We must also use a vertical-unit system which will be the widths of the boards and batten-bands themselves, interlocking with the brick courses. Although it is getting to be a luxury material, the walls will be wood board walls the same inside as outside—three thicknesses of boards with paper placed between them, the boards fastened together with screws. These slab walls of boards—a kind of plywood construction on a large scale—can be high in insulating value, vermin-proof, and practically fireproof. These walls, like the fenestration, may be prefabricated on the floor, with any degree of insulation we can afford, and raised into place, or they may be made at the mill and shipped to the site in sections. The roof can be built first on props and these walls shoved into place under them.

The appurtenance systems, to avoid cutting and complications, must be an organic part of construction but independent of the walls. Yes, we must have polished plate glass. It is one of the things we have at hand to gratify the designer of the truly modern house and bless its occupants.

The roof framing in this instance is laminated of three 2 x 4's one above the other, easily making the three offsets seen outside in the eaves of the roof, and enabling the roof span to be sufficiently pitched without the expense of building up. The middle offset may be left open at the eaves and fitted with flaps to ventilate the roof spaces in summer. These 2 x 4's sheathed and insulated, then covered with a good asphalt roof, are the top of the house, gratifying the sense of shelter because of generous eaves.

All this is in hand—no, it is in mind, as we plan the disposition of the rooms.

What must we consider essential now? We have a corner lot—say an acre or two—with a south and west exposure? We will have a good garden. The house is planned to wrap around two sides of this garden.

1. We must have as big a living room with as much vista and garden coming in as we can afford, with a fireplace in it, and open bookshelves, a dining table in the alcove, benches, and living room tables built in; a quiet rug on the floor.

2. Convenient cooking and dining space adjacent to if not a part of the living room. This space may be set away from the outside walls within the living area to make work easy. This is the new thought concerning a kitchen—to take it away from outside walls and let it up into overhead space within the chimney; thus connection to dining space is made immediate without unpleasant features and no outside wall space lost to the principal rooms. A natural current of air is thus set up toward the kitchen as toward a chimney, no cooking odors escaping back into the house. There are steps leading down to a small cellar below for heater, fuel, and laundry, although no basement at all is necessary if the plan permits. The bathroom is usually next so that plumbing features of heating, kitchen and bath may be economically combined.

3. In this case (two bedrooms and a workshop which may become a future bedroom) the single bathroom, for the sake of privacy, is not immediately connected to any single bedroom. We will have as much garden and space as our money allows after we have simplified construction by way of the techniques described.

As a matter of course a home like this is an architect's creation. It is not a builder's nor an amateur's effort.

A house of this type could not be well built and achieve its design, unless an architect oversees the building.

And the building would fail of proper effect unless furnishing and planting were all done by advice of the architect.

1943a

In either a very cold or a very hot climate, the overhead is where insulation should occur in any building. There you can spend money for insulation with very good effect, whereas the insulation of the walls and the air space within the walls becomes less and less important. With modern systems of air conditioning and heating you can manage almost any condition.

But the best insulation for a roof and walls in a hot climate is nearly the same as the best insulation for a roof and walls in a cold region. Resistance to heat in a building is much the same as resistance to cold, although of course the exact specifications should vary according to circumstances.

In northern climates you can see how well a house is insulated by noticing how quickly the snow melts off the roof. If the snow stays for some time, the roof is pretty well insulated. If you get insulation up to a certain point, snow will come and give you more.

One of the advantages of the sloping roof is that it gives you a sense of spaciousness inside, a sense of uplift which I often feel to be very good. The flat roof has advantages in construction; it is easy to do. But with the flat roof, you must devise ways and means to get rid of water. One way is to build, on top of the flat, a slight pitch to the eaves. This may be done by furring. There are various ways of getting water off a flat roof. But it must be done.

The cheapest roof, however, is the shed roof—the roof sloping one way, more or less. There you get more for your money than you can get from any other form of roof. There is no water problem with a shed roof because the water goes down to the lower side and drops away. With a hip roof the water runs two ways into a natural valley, so there is not much problem there either.

... In the Usonian plan the kitchen is called the workspace and identified largely with the living room. As a matter of fact, it becomes an alcove of the living room, higher for good ventilation and spaciousness. The kitchen being one of the places where smells originate, we made it the ventilating flue of the whole house by carrying it up higher than the living room. All the air from the surrounding house is thus drawn up through the kitchen itself. The same is true of the way the bathrooms are made. We were never by this means able to eliminate noise. So in a Usonian house a needlessly noisy kitchen is a bad thing.

Everything in the Usonian kitchen should be (as it may so easily be) modern and attractive. Because it is incorporated into the living room, the kitchen (workspace) should be just as charming to be in or look at as the living room—
1954a perhaps more so.

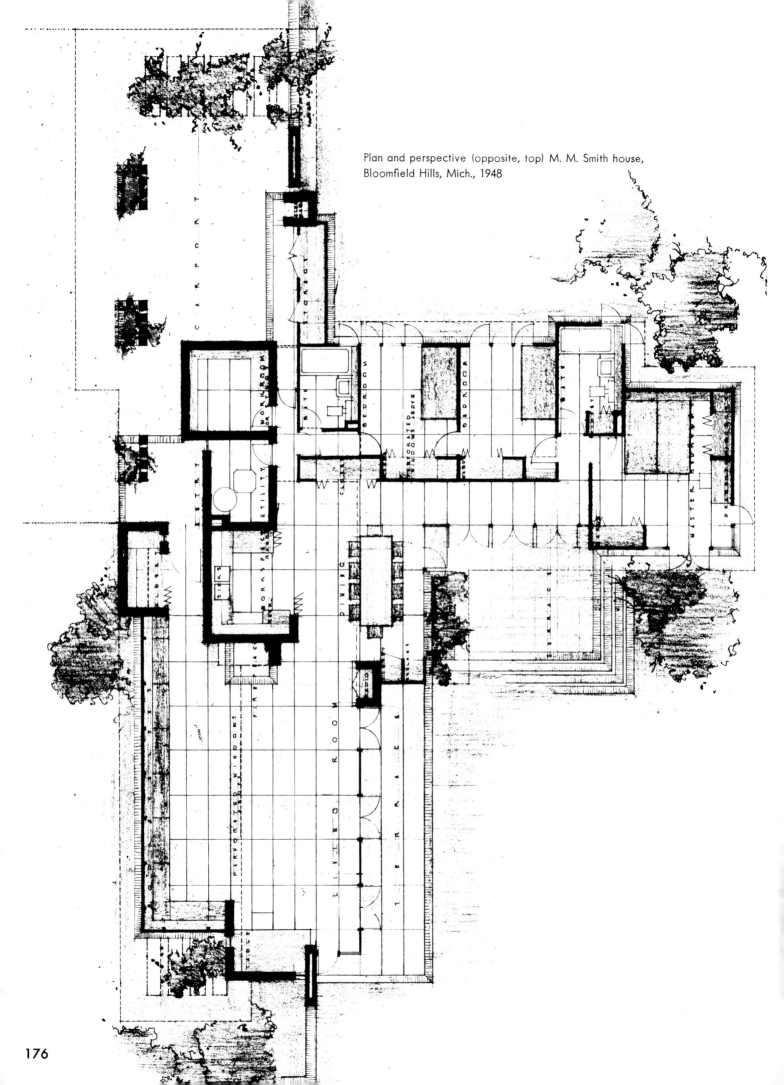

Plan and perspective (opposite, top) M. M. Smith house,
Bloomfield Hills, Mich., 1948

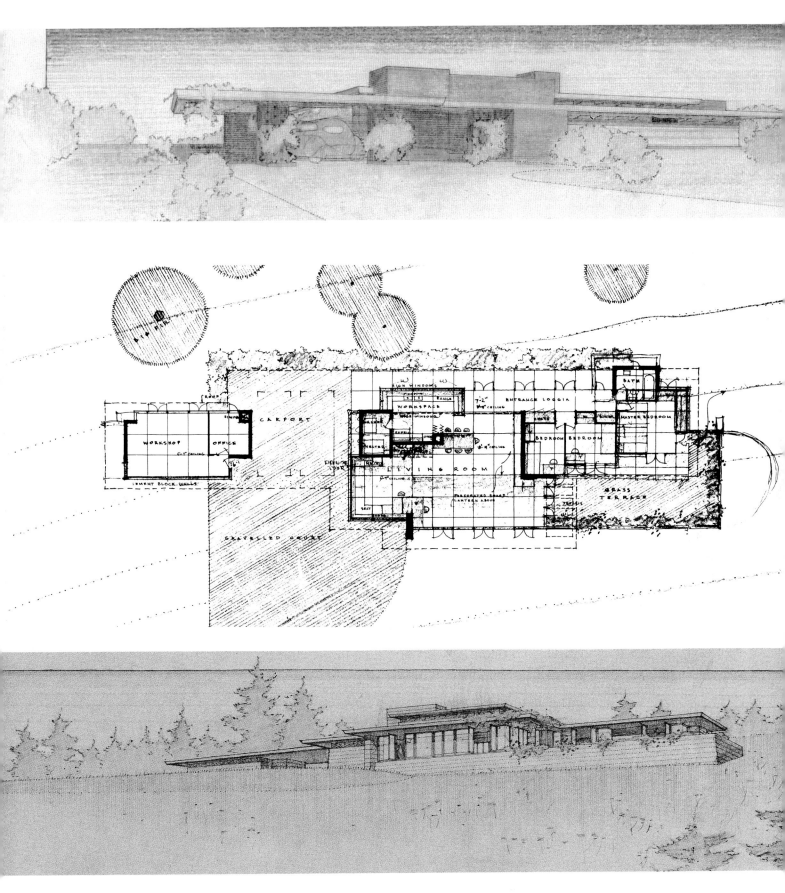

Middle and bottom: plan and perspective,
projected Brandes house, Bellevue, Wash., 1952

THE ZONED HOUSE

New facilities make it desirable to lay aside the provincial American parlor. A beautiful kitchen should now go where the parlor went some time ago. With modern appurtenances what used to be the kitchen can now become a high spacious work studio opening level with the garden, therefore, a natural get-together place in which to live while at work. In a zoned plan the utility stack has, economically standardized and concentrated within it, all appurtenances of modern house construction: oil burning boiler and fuel tanks—air compressors, oil and gasoline supply for car, heating and air conditioning units, electric wiring and plumbing, vent and smoke flues. This enlarged hollow chimney—about 6 by 8 feet on the ground—is accessible from the coat-room and so placed that only one short run of horizontal pipe or wire to the study is necessary. Each bathroom is a one-piece, standardized fixture directly connected to the stack. Kitchen sink, ranges and refrigeration, likewise. Here at the nexus of the arrangement is complete standardized factory production, in lieu of the wasteful, tangled web of wires and piping involved in the construction of the ordinary dwelling at present. Thus the cost of about one third of the usual home is here seen as reduced to a certainty, and one half or one third of the cost is potentially saved.

The carport, integral feature of the dwelling, is convenient, not the gaping hole it usually is. Other features of the zoned house are the utilities stack; the development of the kitchen into the real living room, completely furnished, part of the whole; and the segregated space called the study. A third zone—the slumber zone—is introduced as mezzanine with balcony opening into the living kitchen or work room. While the children are young, each has a dressing room and sleeps out. When they grow up, by a few simple changes in the mezzanine each has a private room. Here are self-contained economies for the family, more natural and more orderly than is possible at present.

This germ-plan would easily adapt itself, as indicated, to the several conditions of the small house in suburb, town and country. The suburban house is shown lighted largely from above—to avoid the more or less indecent exposure most suburban houses suffer from when they try to be little country houses on lots 50 feet

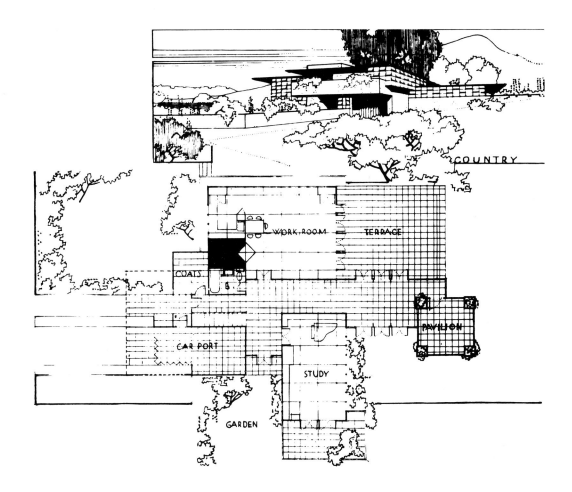

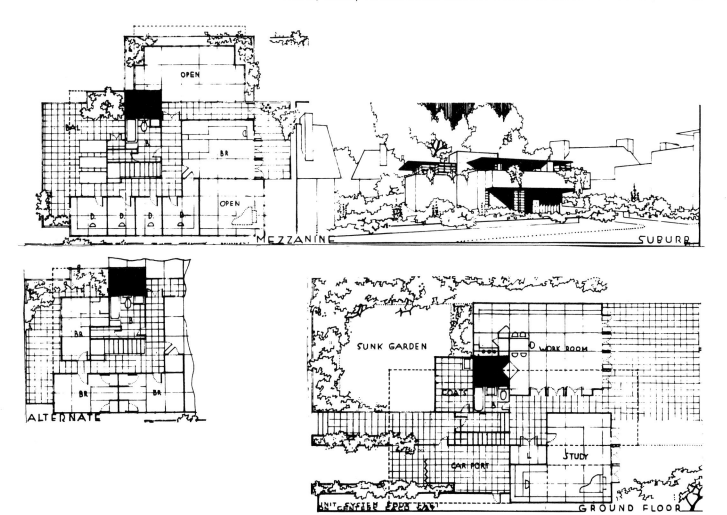

Above, country version; below, suburban version: the Zoned House; project developed 1935

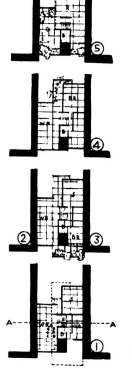

wide. The town house is tall, all rooms having high ceilings. The entire house is hermetically sealed from dirt and noise and air-conditioned, with opportunity to go out to view the passing show on occasions, but only when moved; also opportunity to live outside, up top where greenery can see the sky. The utility stack and bathrooms, work room, segregated study and segregated slumber rooms of this town house all keep to the underlying scheme of the suburban house.

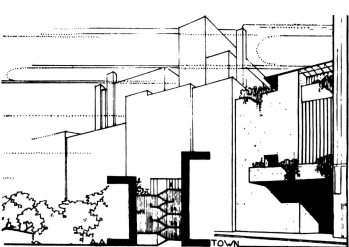

Left, plans; right, section through building: the Zoned House, city version, project developed 1935

The country house has the same scheme too. Its outer walls are mostly metal and glass screens and the plan is opened wide to sun, air and vista. A spreading good-time place is possible in country life.

The designs could utilize different materials by modifying structural details only. The simple exterior we have indicated would lend itself to synthetic sheet materials, to slab construction or to wood frame with plaster. Were brick or stone to be used the walls would be thicker, reducing floor space somewhat without any other changes because the upper story is, in every case, mostly glass and would need the protecting roof planes for protection. The roofs of suburb and country versions also might be utilized as terraces if surroundings and circumstances made it desirable. There is no basement; it has disappeared: the main floor is made directly upon a concrete mat laid over dry filling, well drained.

This zoned suburban house, complete, should not cost over six thousand dollars for garage, three bedrooms, two bathrooms and commodious living areas. Where conditions were favorable and prefabrication possible such a house could come within a four-thousand-dollar cost limit excluding financing charges or large profits.

In a house of this type, the idea of a servant is unsuitable. Outside help—coming at stated times—more professional, should be all the modern housewife would need with modern labor-saving devices and bringing up the young to accept normal responsibilities in the household.

1935a

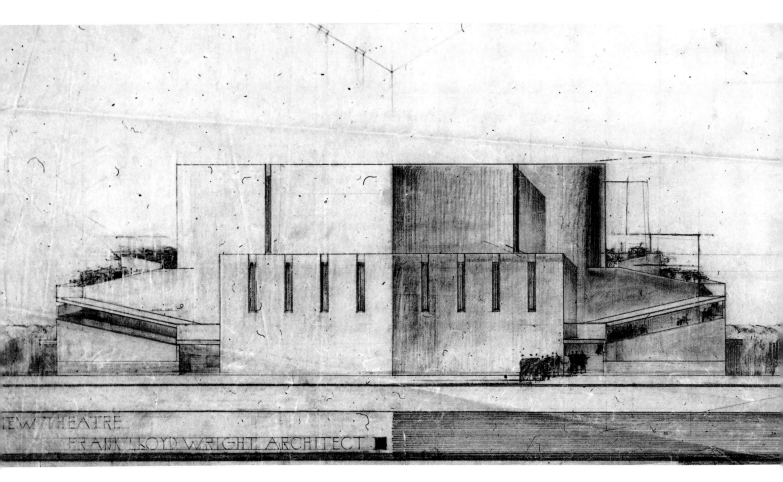

EW THEATRE
FRANK LLOYD WRIGHT ARCHITECT

Front, showing entrance at right side: project for A New Theatre, 1932

THE NEW THEATRE

We do not intend to explain here technical details of the design for the New Theatre. Controversy is inevitable to the new and therefore unfamiliar ways of achieving greater impact of actor upon audience. But the main ideas of such a theatre are clear enough.

181

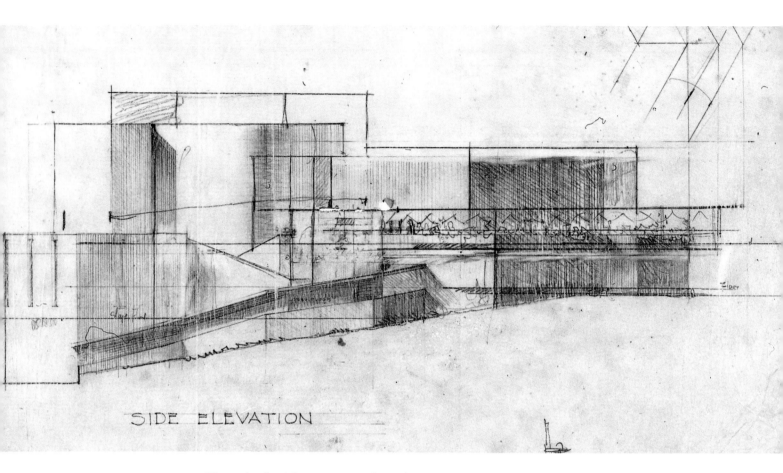

SIDE ELEVATION

Free the legitimate stage from its present peep-show character and scenery loft, establishing a simple, workable basis for presenting plays in the round, performers and audience together in one room, allowing staging more like sculpture than like painting: now a frame (or proscenium) places performance in one room, audience in another.

Playwright and stage designer when familiar with this new freedom will discover fascinating realms of expression open to them; and no doubt the best of them will be inspired to create new dramatic effects.

Actors will find the acoustics of the New Theatre so sensitive that the slightest nuance of tone, or shade of expression, will register with ease and far greater effect than under present conditions.

Lighting and music are provided for. Lighting is such that make-up is more effective; less will be needed.

A production is reduced to simple mechanical means; several men can do work now done by dozens.

Sets are all prepared below stage and rise by way of tracks and dollies on the ramps to become scenery on the revolving stage. By dropping the dividing screen, a great depth may be added to the revolving stage. Scenes can succeed one another almost instantly. A set rises on one ramp and goes back down on the one opposite. If desired, a continuous performance may be staged.

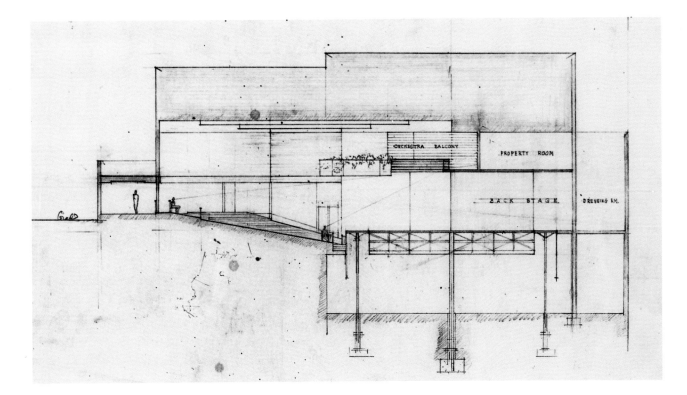

The entire atmosphere or effect of the auditorium and stage taken together dramatizes the performance itself and serves to heighten artistic values by concentration and contrast.

Building construction and arrangements within are fireproof and made with regard to safety and comfort. Entrance is from one side, egress from the other. Directed exits are directly behind the audience, coat rooms and toilets conveniently on main level.

The New Theatre is excellent for orchestral concerts. Lectures or solo performances of every kind.

The technical equipment of the New Theatre may be as desired, more and more detailed until almost automatic. Costs of production could not only be cut but effects made possible that are now impossible.

By means of these simple organic changes in technique and traditions a new life for the theatre is likely.

1949a

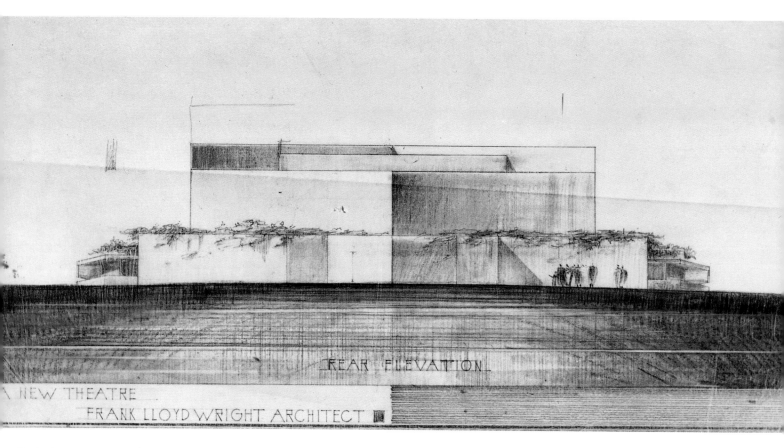

Back elevation: project for A New Theatre, 1932

OUT OF THE GROUND INTO THE LIGHT

"Vegetable life—inexorable—inexhaustible in variety"
Mr. Wright's family farmland landscaped by him

EARTH

All materials lie piled in masses or float as gases in the landscape of this planet much as the cataclysms of creation left them.

At the mercy of the cosmic elements, these materials have been disintegrated by temperatures, ground down by glaciers, eroded by wind and sea, sculptured by tireless forces qualifying each other. They are all externally modified by time as they modify this earth in a ceaseless procession of change.

Stone is the basic material of our planet. It is continually changed by cosmic forces, themselves a form of change. Contrasted with these great mineral masses of earth structure—this titanic wreckage—are placid depths and planes of mutable water or the vast depth-plane of the immutable sky hung with evanescent clouds. And this creeping ground-cover of vegetable life, more inexorable than death, is rising from it all, over all, against all, texturing with pattern, infinite in resource, and inexhaustible in variety of effect. This is the earthly abode of the buildings man has built to work, dwell, worship, dance and breed in.

Change is the one immutable circumstance found in landscape. But the changes all speak or sing in unison of cosmic law, itself a nobler form of change. These cosmic laws are the physical laws of all man-built structures as well as the laws of landscape.

Man takes a positive hand in creation whenever he puts a building upon the earth beneath the sun. If he has birthright at all, it must consist in this: that he, too, is no less a feature of the landscape than the rocks, trees, bears or bees of that nature to which he owes his being.

Continuously nature shows him the science of her remarkable economy of structure in mineral and vegetable constructions to go with the unspoiled character everywhere apparent in her forms.

The long, low lines of colorful, windswept terrain, the ineffable dotted line, the richly textured plain, great striated, stratified masses lying noble and quiet or rising with majesty above the vegetation of the desert floor: nature-masonry is piled up into ranges upon ranges of mountains that seem to utter a form language of their own.

To what end is all in pattern?

Always—eternally—pattern? Why?

Why this intrigue of eye-music to go with sensuous ear-music?

What is this inner realm of rhythm that dances in sentient beings and lies quiescent but no less sentient in pattern?

There seems to be no mortal escape, least of all in death, from this earth-principle which is again the sun-principle of growth. Earth becomes more and more the creative creature of the sun. It is a womb quickened by the passions of the master sun.

Nevertheless, every line and the substance of earth's rock-bound structure speak of violence. All is scarred by warring forces seeking reconciliation, still marred by conflict and conquest. But in our era violence has subsided, is giving way to comparative repose. Streamlines of the mountain ranges come down more gently to the plains. Geological cataclysm is subsiding or becoming subservient. Divine order creeps out and rises superior to chaos. Pattern asserts itself. Once more, triumph.

Ceaselessly, the rock masses are made by fire, are laid low by water, are sculptured by wind and stream. They take on the streamlines characteristic of the

Taliesin West in the desert   sweeping forces that change them.

Already matter lies quieted, and with it violence and discord. It is bathed in light that so far as man can see is eternal. Penetrating all, itself penetrated by itself, is mysterious eye-music: pattern.

1937a

WISCONSIN

More dramatic elsewhere, perhaps more strange, more thrilling, more grand, too, but nothing that picks you up in its arms and so gently, almost lovingly, cradles you as do these southwestern Wisconsin hills. These ranges of low hills

A Taliesin landscape

that make these fertile valleys of southwestern Wisconsin by leading down to the great sandy plain that was once the bed of a mightier Wisconsin river than any of us have ever seen.

I doubt if that vast river flood were more beautiful then, however, than this wide, slow-winding, curving stream in the broad sand bed, where gleaming sand-bars make curved beaches and shaded shores to be overhung by masses of great greenery. Well, it is not quite like any of the more important rivers of the world. It is more what specialists in scenery would call picturesque. It is, however, unique.

So human is this countryside in scale and feeling. Pastoral beauty, I believe, the poets call it. More like Tuscany, perhaps, than any other land, but the Florentines that roamed those hills never saw such wild flowers as we see any spring, if the snow has been plentiful. The snow usually is plentiful and the cold too.   1932d

... The buildings became a brow for the hill itself. The strata of fundamental stonework kept reaching around and on into the four courts, and made them. Then stone, stratified, went into the lower house walls and up from the ground itself into the broad chimneys. This native stone prepared the way for the lighter plastered construction of the upper wooden walls. Taliesin was to be an abstract combination of stone and wood as they naturally met in the aspect of the hills around about. And the lines of the hills were the lines of the roofs, the slopes of the hills their slopes, the plastered surfaces of the light wooden walls, set back into shade beneath broad eaves, were like the flat stretches of sand in the river below and the same in color, for that is where the material that covered them came from.   1932a

I wanted a home where icicles by invitation might beautify the eaves. So there were no gutters. And when the snow piled deep on the roofs and lay drifted in the courts, icicles came to hang staccato from the eaves. Prismatic crystal pendants sometimes six feet long, glittered between the landscape and the eyes inside. Taliesin in winter was a frosted palace roofed and walled with snow, hung with iridescent fringes, the plate glass of the windows shone bright and warm through it all as the light of the huge fireplaces lit them from the firesides within, and streams of wood smoke from a dozen such places went straight up toward the stars.   1932a

"The buildings became a brow for the hill itself"
Taliesin, house and land

"More like Tuscany, perhaps, than any other land". Bridge over stream at Taliesin

"Umbrageous architecture—eaves perforated to allow sunlight to penetrate"
Coonley playhouse, Riverside, Ill., 1912

Unity Temple, Oak Park, Ill., 1905

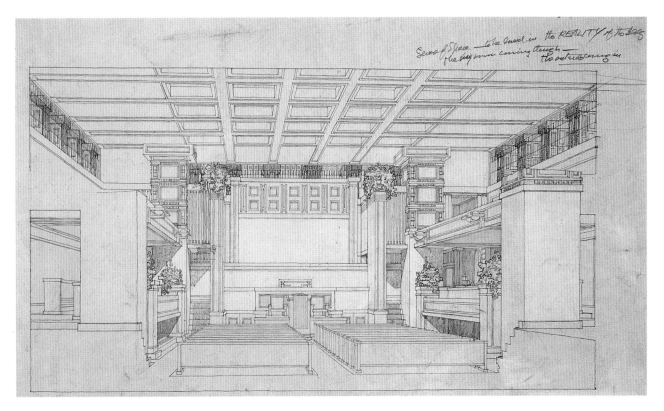

Interior perspective, Unity Temple

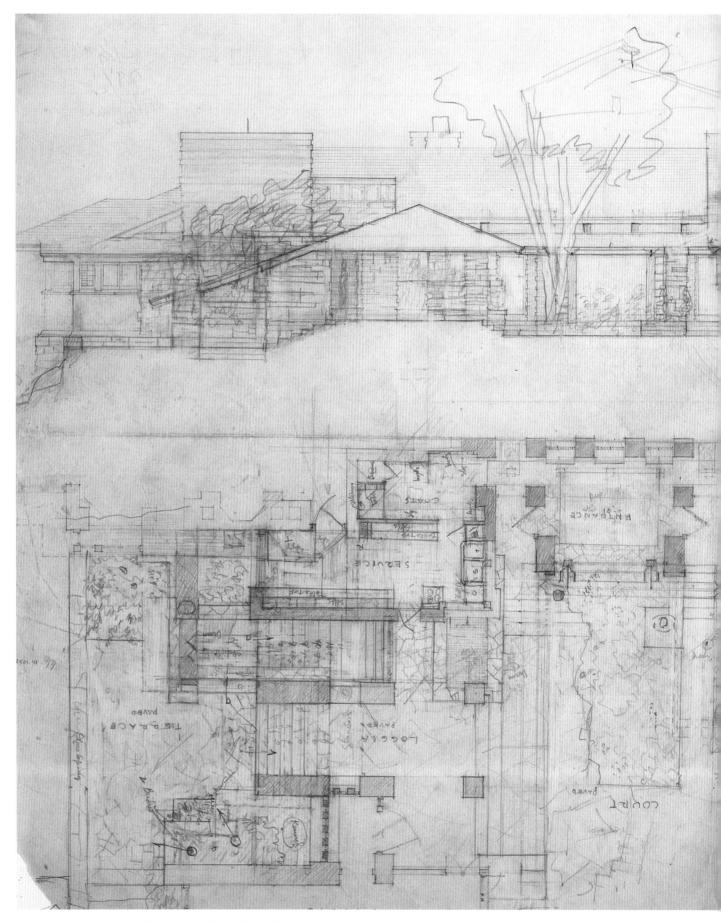

Elevation and floorplan, Taliesin East, Spring Green, Wis., 1925

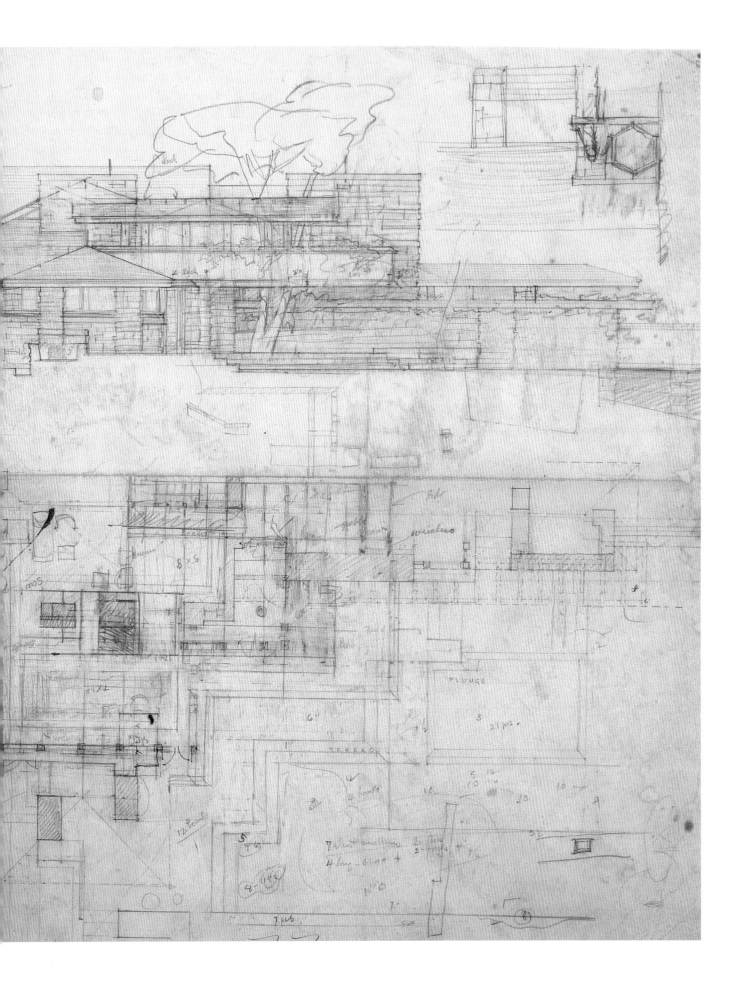

Interior perspective, S. C. Johnson & Son Company administrative building, Racine, Wis., 1936

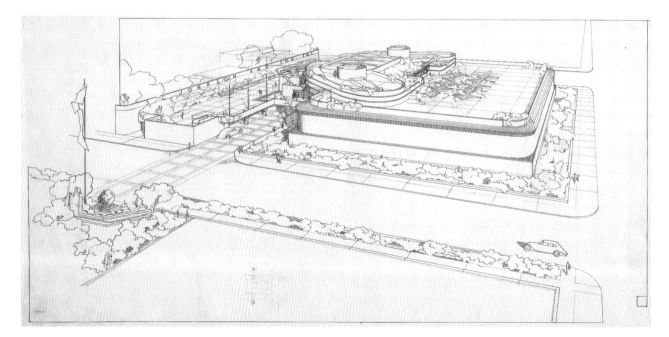

S. C. Johnson & Son Company administrative building

Interior perspective, H. F. Johnson house, "Wingspread," Wind Point, Wis., 1937

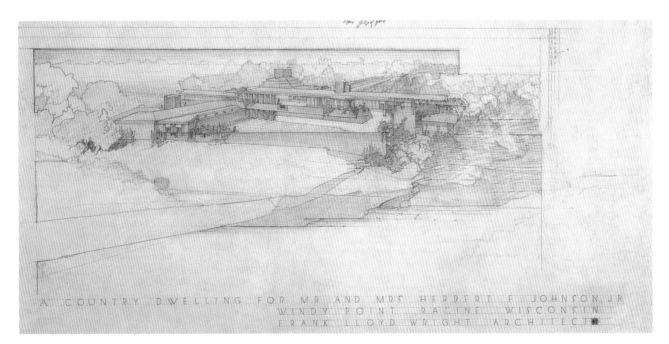

Perspective, H. F. Johnson house

Cooperative Homesteads, Detroit, Mich., 1942: project

Interior perspective, Cooperative Homesteads

"Cloverleaf," quadruple housing, Pittsfield, Mass., 1942: project

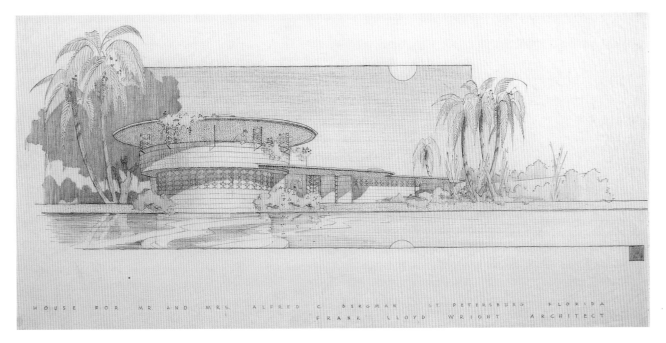

Bergman house, St. Petersburg, Fla., 1948: project

"San Marcos-in-the-Desert," resort hotel, Chandler, Ariz., 1928: project

Interior perspective, "San Marcos-in-the-Desert"

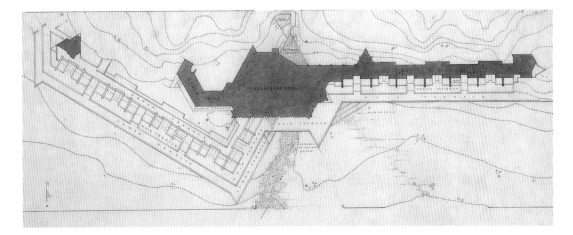

Floorplan, "San Marcos-in-the-Desert"

THE NEW THEATER
DALLAS THEATER CENTER
FRANK LLOYD WRIGHT   ARCHITECT

Kalita Humphreys Theater, Dallas, Tex., 1955

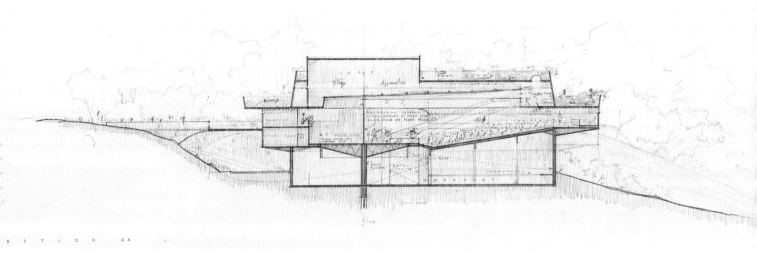

Section, Kalita Humphreys Theater

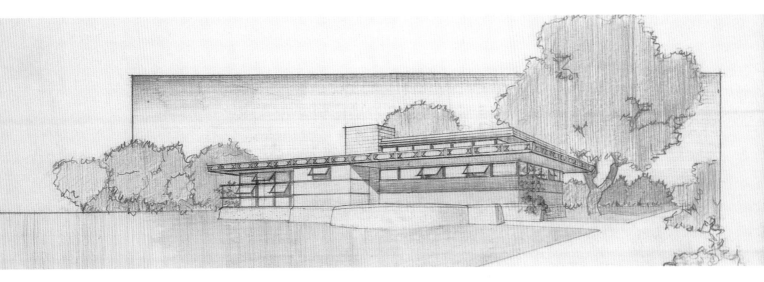

Prefabricated house for Marshall Erdman, scheme #3, Madison, Wis., 1959: project

RESIDENCE FOR DR & MRS JOHN J DOBKINS · CANTON, OHIO
FRANK LLOYD WRIGHT ARCHITECT

Dobkins house, Canton, Ohio, 1953

FROM TOWER

PLANS FOR THE ROGERS LACY

Perspective from tower, Rogers Lacy Hotel, Dallas, Tex., 1946: project

VIEW FROM NORTHWEST
POINT VIEW RESIDENCES
FOR THE EDGAR J. KAUFMANN CHARITABLE TRUST
FRANK LLOYD WRIGHT ARCHITECT SHEET

"Point View Residences," apartment tower, scheme #2, Pittsburgh, Pa., 1953: project

XIII

Mural, Midway Gardens, Chicago, Ill., 1913

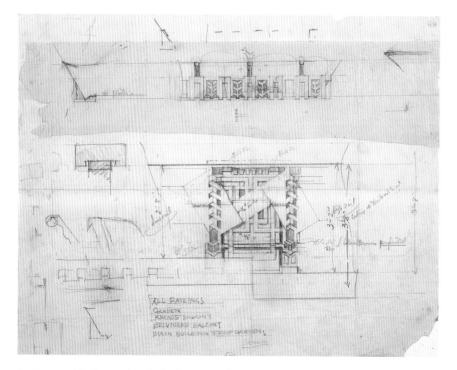

Railing and Balcony detail, Midway Gardens

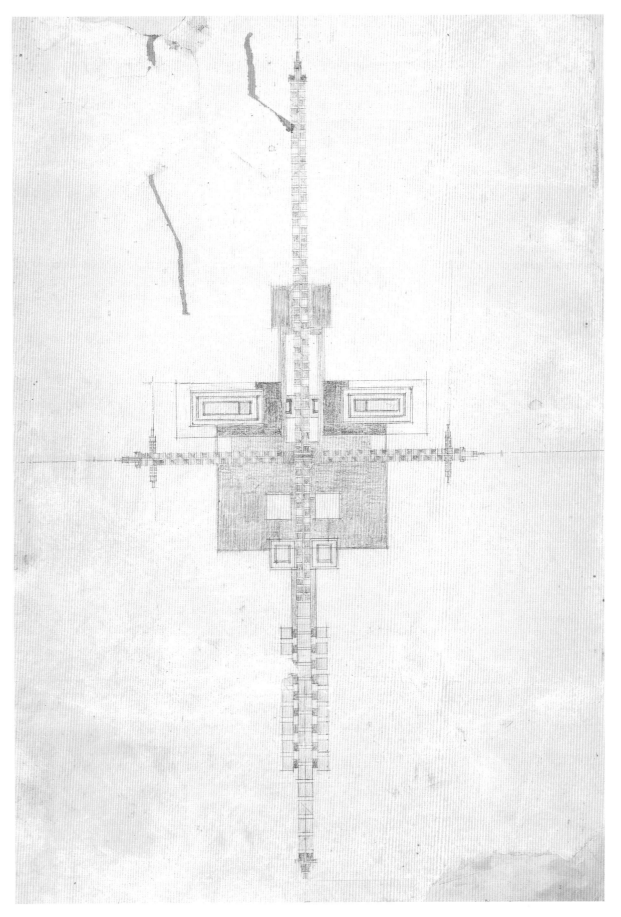

Rug design, Bogk house, Milwaukee, Wis., 1916

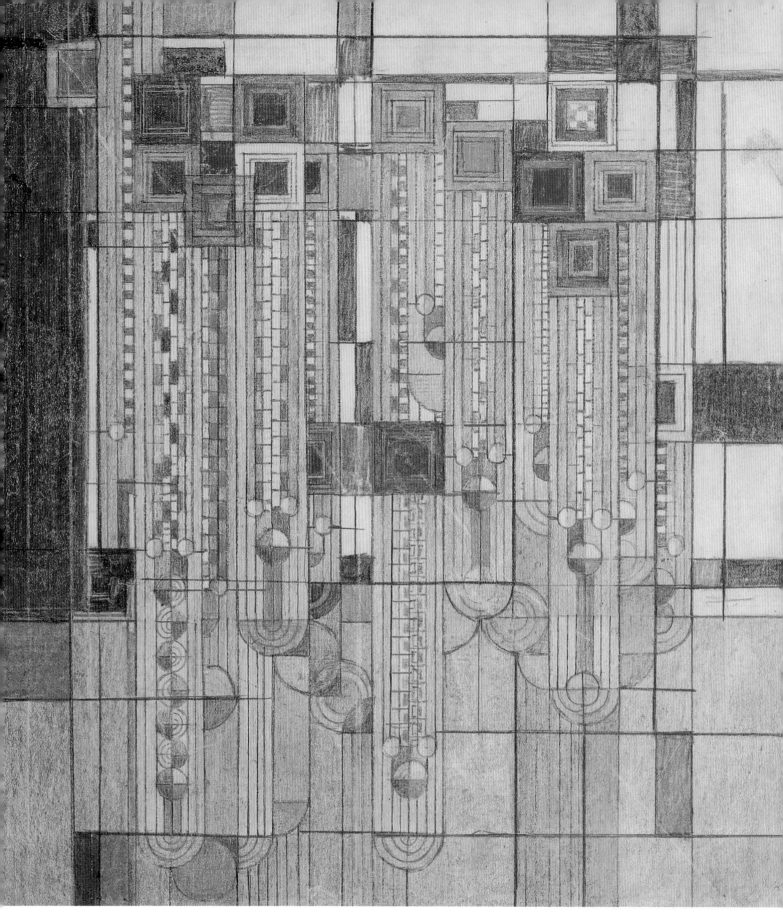

"Saguaro Forms and Cactus Flowers," cover design for *Liberty Magazine*, New York, N.Y., 1926: project

PRAIRIE

I loved the prairie by instinct as, itself, a great simplicity; the trees, flowers, and sky were thrilling by contrast. And I saw that a little of height on the prairie was enough to look like much more. Notice how every detail as to height becomes intensely significant and how breadths all fall short.

In considering the various forms and types of these structures, the fact that nearly all were buildings for our vast Western prairie should be borne in mind; the gently rolling or level prairies of our great Middle West; the great rolling prairies where every detail of elevation becomes exaggerated; every tree towers above the great calm plains of flowered surfaces as the plain lies serene beneath a wonderful unlimited sweep of sky. The natural tendency of every ill-considered thing on the prairie is to detach itself and stick out like a sore thumb in surroundings by nature perfectly quiet. All unnecessary heights have for that reason and the human scale (for other reasons too, economic) been eliminated. More intimate relation with outdoor environment and far-reaching vista is sought to balance the desired lessening of height.

1936a

In our vast country alternate violent extremes of heat and cold, of sun and storm, have to be considered. In the North frost goes four feet into the ground in winter while in summer the sun beats fiercely on the roofs with almost tropical heat. Umbrageous architecture is therefore desirable—almost a necessity both to shade the building from the sun and protect the walls from alternate freezing and thawing. Changes of temperature are more rapidly destructive to buildings than almost all other natural causes. Overhanging eaves, however, leave the house in winter without necessary sun, and this is overcome by the way in which the window groups in certain rooms and exposures are pushed out to the gutter line or eaves perforated to allow sunlight to penetrate. Gently sloping roofs on most of these houses are grateful to the prairie on which they stand as well as to the hills and valleys. They also leave insulating air spaces above the rooms. The chimney has grown and is still growing in dimensions and importance. The kitchen also. In hot weather both features ventilate the whole edifice, being high. Circulating air spaces beneath the roofs are also included, fresh air entering beneath the eaves through openings easily closed in winter.

Conductor rain pipes, disfiguring downspouts, particularly where eaves overhang, freeze in this climate, become useless in winter or burst with disastrous results. So concrete rain-basins are built on the ground level beneath the outer corners of the eaves. Roof water drops down through open spouts in the eaves into their concave surfaces to be conducted to a cistern by underground drain tiles.

Another modern opportunity is afforded by our effective system of hot water heating. By this means the forms of buildings may be more completely articulated: light, air and view had on several sides. By keeping ceilings generally low in cold climates the walls may be opened with series of windows to the outer air and the surrounding flowers and trees, to the general prospects, so one may live with a greater sense of space as comfortably as formerly but much less shut in. Many of these structures carry this principle of space and articulation of various parts to the point where each room has its own individuality and its use completely recognized in the floor plan. Dining room, kitchen and sleeping rooms thus may become small buildings in themselves. All are grouped together to form a whole, as in the Coonley house. It is also possible to spread the buildings (which once upon a time in our climate of extremes were joined in a compact box cut into

compartments) and expand them into a more spacious expression of organic space
—making a house in a garden or in the country the delightful thing that fresh
1910a imagination would have it in relation to either.

"Each room has its own individuality and its use completely recognized in floor plan"
Martin and Barton houses, Buffalo, N. Y., 1903, 1904

DESERT

Out here in the great spaces obvious symmetry claims too much, I find, wearies the eye too soon and stultifies the imagination. Obvious symmetry usually closes the episode before it begins. So for me I felt there could be no obvious symmetry in any building in this great desert. . . .

Arizona character seems to cry out for a space-loving architecture of its own. The straight line and flat plane must come here—of all places—but they should become the dotted line, the broad, low, extended plane textured, because in all this astounding desert there is not one hard undotted line to be seen. The great nature-masonry we see rising from the great mesa floors is . . . not architecture at all, but it is inspiration. A pattern of what appropriate Arizona architecture might well be, lies there hidden in the sahuaro: the sahuaro, perfect example of rein-forced building construction. Its interior vertical rods held it rigidly upright maintaining its great fluted columnar mass for six centuries or more. A truer skyscraper than we have yet built.

And all these remarkable desert growths show economy in their patterns of construction; the stalks especially teach any architect or engineer who is modest and intelligent enough to apply for lessons. In these desert constructions he may not only see the reinforcing-rod "scientifically" employed as in the flesh of the sahuaro but he may see the perfect lattice or the reed and "welded" tubular construction in the stalk of the cholla, or staghorn, and see it too in the cellular build-up of the water barrel, bignana. Even the flesh of the prickly pear is worth studying for its structure. In most cacti nature employs cell-to-cell or continuous tubular or often plastic construction. By means of plasticity nature makes continuity everywhere strongly effective.

Yes, desert is rock-bound earth prostrate to the sun. All life there above the crystal is tenacious sun-life. All life there dies a sun-death. Evidence is everywhere, sometimes ghastly.

It is gratifying as we look around us to see how well we fit into this strange, Taliesin West, Scottsdale, Ariz., 1938 stern, well-armed, creeping cover of abstract land and its peculiar growth, almost as abstract. This inexorable grasp of growing vegetation upon the earth itself is more terrifying to me as a principle at work than what we call death. Growth is everywhere more terrible and terrifying to me than all the other evidences of inexorable force put together.

There seems to be no mortal escape, especially not in death, from this inexorable earth-principle—or is it sun-principle—of growth: this creative creature of the great sun?

And what of the subsidence we see now in the streamlines of these endless ranges of mountains coming gently down to the mesa or going abruptly up into the sky from the plains. In this geologic era, catastrophic upheaval has found comparative repose; to these vast, quiet, ponderable masses made so by fire and laid by water—both are architects—now comes the sculptor, wind. Wind and water ceaselessly eroding, endlessly working to quiet and harmonize all traces of violence until a glorious unison is again bathed in the atmosphere of a light that is, it must be, eternal.

1932a

A desert building should be nobly simple in outline as the region itself is sculptured: should have learned from the cactus many secrets of straight line patterns for its forms, playing with the light and softening the building into its proper place among the organic desert creations—the manmade building heightening the beauty of the desert and the desert more beautiful because of the building.

Anyone may see that the desert abhors sun-defiance as nature abhors a vacuum. This universal sun-acceptance by way of pattern is a condition of survival and is everywhere evident. That means integral ornament in everything. Sun-acceptance in building means dotted outlines and wall-surfaces that eagerly take the light and play with it, break it up and render it harmless or drink it in until sunlight blends the building into place with the creation around it.

1940a

Pool and terrace at Taliesin West, Scottsdale, Ariz., 1938

"A desert building should be nobly simple in outline as the region itself is sculptured"
Taliesin West, Scottsdale, Ariz., 1938

Entrance court at Taliesin West, Scottsdale, Ariz., 1938

"Architectural association accentuates the character of landscape"
Walter boathouse, Quasqueton, Iowa, 1949

SITE

My prescription for a modern house: first, a good site. Pick that one at the most difficult spot—pick a site no one wants—but pick one that has features making for character: trees, individuality, a fault of some kind in the realtor mind. That now means getting out of the city. Then, standing on that site, look about you so that you see what has charm. What is the reason you want to build there? Find out. Then build your house so that you may still look from where you stood upon all that charmed you and lose nothing of what you saw before the house was built but see more. Architectural association accentuates the character of landscape 1938b if the architecture is right.

No one noticed that it was a particularly beautiful site until the house was built. Then as the depth-planes came into play they began to realize how beautiful it really was. When organic architecture is properly carried out no landscape is ever outraged by it but is always developed by it. 1939a

"A good site . . . at the most difficult spot . . . one that has features . . . individuality"
La Miniatura, Pasadena, Cal., 1923

WHERE PRINCIPLE IS PUT TO WORK

THERE WILL ALWAYS BE STYLE: I

CONTINUITY

Classic architecture was all fixation-of-the-fixture. Yes, entirely so. Now why not let walls, ceilings, floors become seen as component parts of each other, their surfaces flowing into each other. . . .

1932a

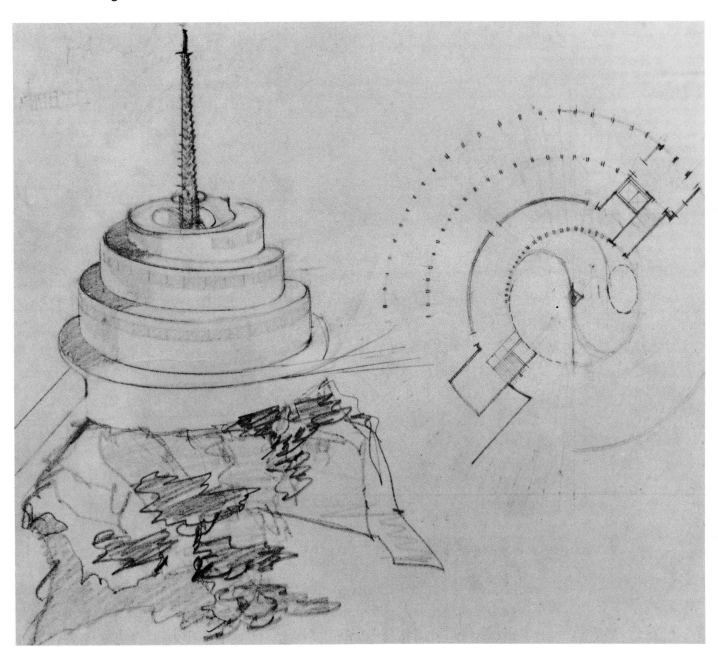

"Let walls, ceilings, floors become seen as component parts of each other, their surfaces flowing into each other"
Aerial perspective and plan, Gordon Strong planetarium project, Sugar Loaf Mountain, Md., 1925

Continuity in this aesthetic sense appeared to me as the natural means to achieve truly organic architecture by machine technique or by any other natural technique. Here was direct means, the only means I could then see or can now see to express, objectify and again bring natural form to architecture. Here by instinct at first (all ideas germinate) principle had entered into building as the new aesthetic, *continuity*.

1936a

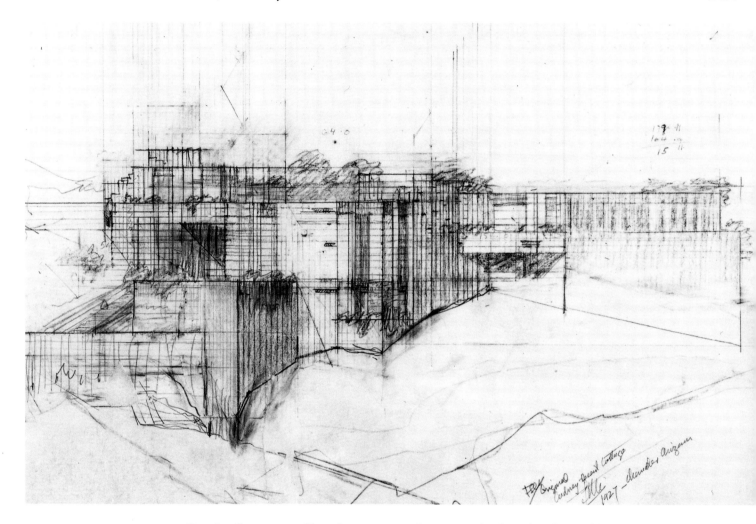

Gradually proceeding from generals to particulars in the field of work with materials and machines continuity began to grip me and work its own will in architecture. I would watch sequences fascinated, seeing other sequences in those consequences already in evidence. I occasionally look through such early studies as I made at this period (a number of them still remain), fascinated by implications. They seem, even now, generic.

Visions of simplicities so broad and far-reaching would open to me and such building harmonies appear, that I was tireless in search of new ones. In various form researches, with all my energy I concentrated upon the principle of plasticity working as continuity. Soon a practical working technique evolved and a new scale within the buildings I was building, in the endeavor to accomplish more

"Even now, generic"
Original sketch of project for Cudney desert cottage near Chandler, Ariz., 1927

"So broad and far-reaching"
Gordon Strong planetarium project, Sugar Loaf Mountain, Md., 1925

sensibly and sensitively this thing we call architecture. Here at work was something that would change and deepen the thinking and culture of the modern world. So I believed.

... Rising to greater dignity as idea, the ideal of plasticity was now to be developed and emphasized in the treatment of the building as a whole. Plasticity was a familiar term but something I had seen in no buildings whatsoever. I had seen it in Lieber Meister's (Louis Sullivan) ornament only; it had not found its way into his buildings otherwise. It might now be seen gradually coming into the expressive lines and surfaces of the buildings I was building. You may see the appearance of the thing in the surface of your hand contrasted with the articulation of the bony skeleton itself. This ideal, profound in its architectural implications, soon took another conscious stride forward in the form of a new aesthetic. I called it *continuity*. It is easy to see it in the folded plane.

Covered walk, Fallingwater, Bear Run, Pa., 1939

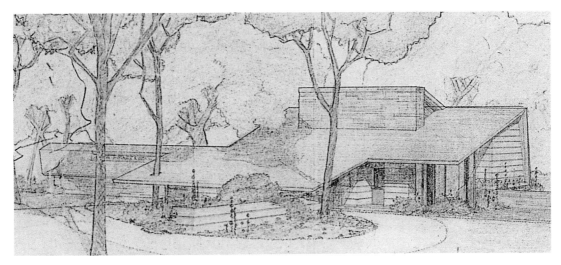

Above, perspective; below, south, east and west elevations: project for Slater house, Warwick, R. I., 1945

I promoted plasticity as conceived by Lieber Meister to *continuity* in the concept of the building as a whole. If the dictum, form follows function, had any bearing at all on building it could take form in architecture only by means of plasticity when seen at work as complete *continuity*. So why not throw away entirely all implications of post and beam construction? Have no posts, no columns, no pilasters, cornices or moldings or ornament; no divisions of the sort nor allow any fixtures whatever to enter as something added to the structure. Any building should be complete, including all within itself. Instead of many things, *one* thing.

"The folded plane enters here emphasized by lines merging wall and ceiling into one . . . continuity in all"

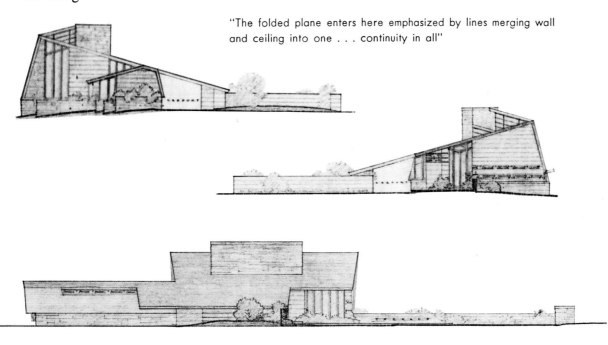

The folded plane enters here emphasized by lines merging wall and ceiling into one. Let walls, ceilings, floors now become not only party to each other but *part of each other,* reacting upon and within one another; continuity in all, eliminating any merely constructed features, fixtures or appliances whatsoever as such.

When Louis Sullivan had eliminated background in his system of ornament in favor of an integral sense of the whole, he had implied this larger sense of the thing. I now began to achieve it.

Conceive that here came a new sense of building on American soil that could *grow* building forms not only true to function but expressive far beyond mere function in the realm of the human spirit. Our new country might now have a true architecture hitherto unknown. Yes, architectural forms by this interior means might now grow up to express a deeper sense of human life-values than any existing before. Architecture might extend the bounds of human individuality indefinitely by way of safe interior discipline. Not only had space come upon a new technique of its own but every material and every method might now speak for itself in objective terms of human life. Architects were no longer tied to Greek space but were free to enter into the space of Einstein.

1936a

But later on I found that in the effort to actually eliminate the post and beam in favor of structural continuity, that is to say, make two things one instead of separate, I could get no help at all from regular engineers. By habit, the engineer reduced everything in the field of calculation to the post and the beam resting upon it before he could calculate and tell you where and just how much for either. He had no other data. Walls made one with floors and ceilings, merging together yet reacting upon each other, the engineer had never met. And the engineer has not yet enough scientific formulae to enable him to calculate for continuity. Floor slabs stiffened and extended as cantilevers over centered supports, as a waiter's tray rests upon his upturned fingers, such as I now began to use in order to get planes parallel to the earth to emphasize the third dimension, were new, as I used them, especially in the Imperial Hotel. But the engineer soon mastered the element of continuity in floor slabs, with such formulae as he had. The cantilever thus became a new feature of design in architecture. As used in the Imperial Hotel at Tokyo it was the most important of the features of construction that insured the life of that

"To emphasize the third dimension"
Imperial Hotel, Tokyo, Japan, 1915-22

building in the terrific temblor of 1922. So, here came not only a new aesthetic, but, the aesthetic now proven scientifically sound, a great new economic stability derived from steel in tension was able to enter building construction.

Where the beam leaves off and the post begins is no longer important, nor need it be seen at all because it no longer actually is. Steel in tension enables the support to slide into the supported, or the supported to grow into the support, somewhat as a tree branch glides out of its tree trunk. Therefrom arises the new series of interior physical reactions I call continuity. As natural consequence, the new aesthetic is no longer a mere appearance: plasticity actually becomes the normal countenance, the true aesthetic of genuine structural reality. Interwoven steel strands may lie in so many directions in any member that all extensions may be economical of material, much lighter, yet safer in construction than ever before. There as in the branch of the tree you may see the cantilever. The cantilever is the simplest of the important phases of this new structural resource, now demanding new significance. It has yet had little attention in architecture. It can do remarkable things to liberate space.

In the form of the cantilever, as horizontal continuity, this new economy saved the Imperial Hotel from destruction.

"More suited to human to and fro than the right angle"
Plan of Vigo Sundt house project, Madison, Wis., 1941

Later, in the new design for St. Mark's Tower, New York City, this new working principle promised to economize material, labor, and liberate space. It gave the structure significant outlines of remarkable stability instead of false masonry-mass. The abstract pattern of the structure as an integrity of form and idea may be seen fused, as in any tree, but with nothing imitating a tree.

1932a

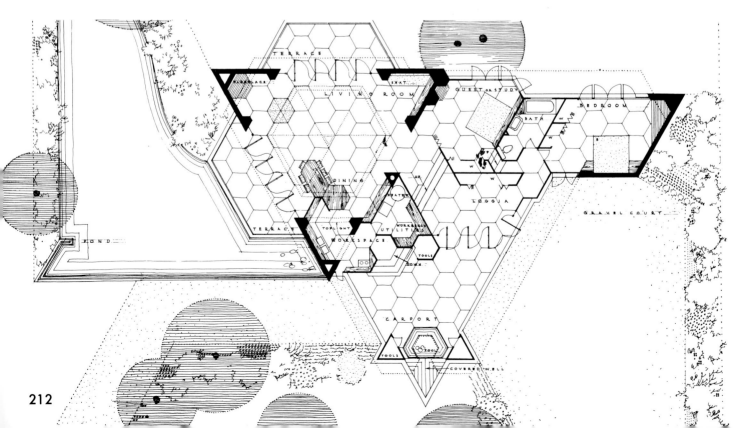

I am convinced that the pattern made by a cross section of honeycomb has more fertility and flexibility where human movement is concerned than the square. The obtuse angle is more suited to human to and fro than the right angle. Flow

"Flow and movement"
Framing, Hanna house, Palo Alto, Cal., 1937

and movement is, in this design, a characteristic lending itself admirably to life, as life is to be lived in it. In the Hanna house the hexagon has been conservatively

treated, however. It is allowed to appear in plan only and in the furniture which literally rises from and befits the floor pattern of the concrete slab upon which the whole stands.

1938a

214

Living room, Hanna house, Palo Alto, Cal., 1937

Guggenheim Museum, New York, N. Y., project begun 1943

The proposed new building for the Guggenheim Museum is the latest sense of organic architecture. Here we are not building a cellular composition of compartments, but one where all is one great space on a single continuous floor.

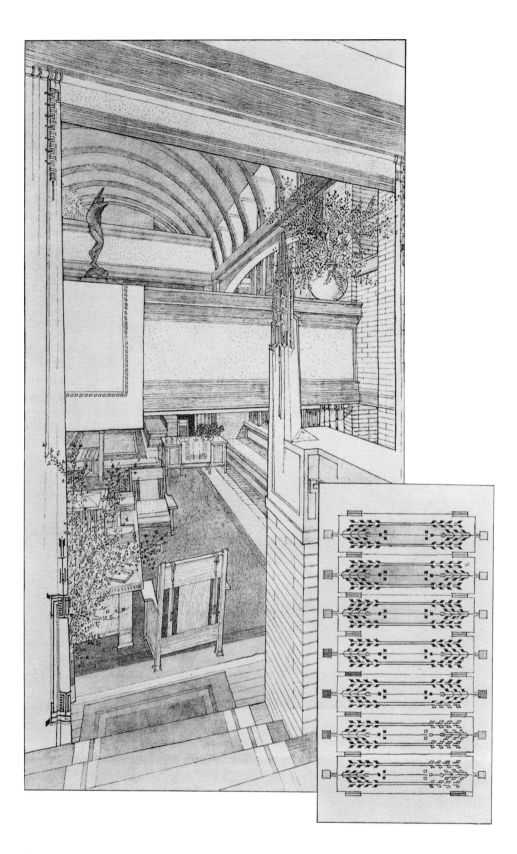

"In integral architecture the room-space itself must come through"
Gallery, Dana house, Springfield, Ill., 1903

The eye encounters no abrupt change, but is gently led and treated as if at the edge of the shore watching an unbreaking wave—or is that too fancy a phrase?

1953a

Here for the first time architecture appears plastic, one floor flowing into another instead of the usual superimposition of stratified layers cutting and butting into each other by post and beam construction.

The whole is cast in concrete more an eggshell in form than a crisscross stick structure. The concrete is rendered strong enough everywhere to do its work by filaments of steel, separate or in mesh. Structural calculations are thus those of cantilever and continuity rather than the conventional post and beam formula. The net result of such construction is greater repose, an atmosphere of the unbroken wave—no meeting of the eye with angular or abrupt changes of form. All is as one and as near indestructible as it is possible to make a building.

1952b

INTERIOR SPACE COMES THROUGH

The interior space itself is the reality of the building. The room itself must come through or architecture has not arrived in the modern sense.

1931a

Architecture now becomes integral, the expression of a new-old reality: the livable interior space of the room itself. In integral architecture the room-space itself must come through. The room must be seen as architecture, or we have no architecture. We have no longer an outside as outside. We have no longer an outside and an inside as two separate things. Now the outside may come inside, and the inside may and does go outside. They are of each other. Form and function thus become one in design and execution if the nature of materials and method and purpose are all in unison.

1932a

... Now came clear *an entirely new sense of architecture,* a higher conception of architecture: architecture not alone as form following function, but conceived as space enclosed. The enclosed space itself might now be seen as the reality of the building. This sense of the within, or the room itself, or the rooms themselves, I now saw as the great thing to be expressed as *architecture.* This sense of interior space made exterior as architecture transcended all that had gone before, made all

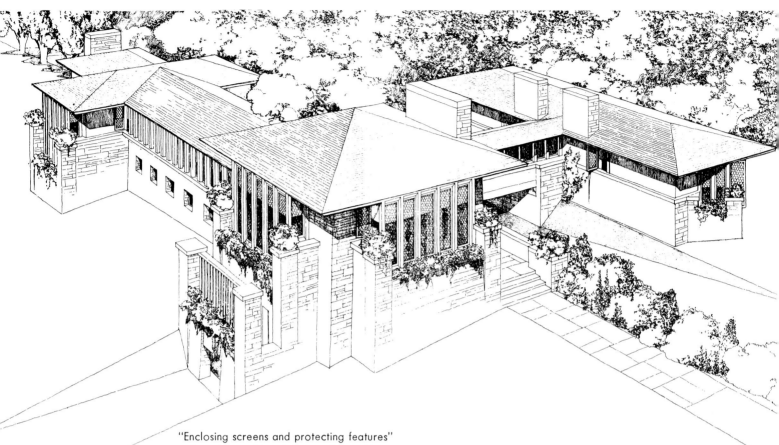

"Enclosing screens and protecting features"
Hillside Home School, Spring Green, Wis., 1902

the previous ideas only useful now as means to the realization of a far greater ideal. Hitherto all classical or ancient buildings had been great masses or blocks of building material, sculptured into shape outside and hollowed out to live in. At least that was the sense of it all. But here coming to light was a sense of building as an organism that had new release for the opportunities of the machine age. This interior conception took architecture entirely away from sculpture, away from painting and entirely away from architecture as it had been known in the antique. The building now became a creation of interior space in light. And as this sense of the interior space as the reality of the building began to work, walls as walls fell away. The vanishing wall joined the disappearing cave. Enclosing screens and protecting features of architectural character took the place of the solid wall.

1931c

Let us go back, here, to the first self-conscious assertion of the third dimension in building, as it came to be called. The reality of the building is not in the four walls and roof but in the space enclosed by them to be lived in. Earlier than this I had been trying to bring the room through. But in Unity Temple (1904-1905) to bring the room through was consciously a main objective. So Unity Temple has no actual walls as walls. Utilitarian features, the stair-enclosures at the corners; low masonry screens carrying roof supports; the upper part of the structure on four sides a continuous window beneath the ceiling of the big room, the ceiling extending out over them to shelter them; the opening of this slab where it passed over the big room to let sunlight fall where deep shadow had been deemed "religious"; these were to a great extent the means employed to achieve the purpose. Since then the "new" concept of building (expressed by Laotze, 500 B.C.) has never slept. You will find it working in many different ways in all the structures shown in this col-

1938a lection, often seeming contradictory.

This sense of the within, the room itself (or the rooms themselves) I see as the great thing to be realized, that may take the new forms we need as architecture.

1936a Such a source would never stultify itself as a mere style.

"The thing to be realized"
Walter house, Quasqueton,
Iowa, 1949

INTEGRAL ORNAMENT

At last, this resource, so old yet now demanding fresh significance. We have arrived at integral ornament—the nature-pattern of actual construction. Here, confessed as the spiritual demand for true significance, comes this subjective element in modern architecture. An element so hard to understand that modern architects themselves seem to understand it least well of all, and most of them have turned against it with such fury as is born only of impotence.

And it is true that this vast, intensely human significance is really no matter at all for any but the most imaginative mind not without some development in artistry and the gift of a sense of proportion. Certainly we must go higher in the realm of imagination when we presume to enter here, because we go into *poetry.*

. . . Imagination giving natural pattern to structure itself. Here we have new significance, indeed! Long ago this significance was lost to the scholarly architect—a man of taste—he, too soon, became content with symbols.

. . . Integral ornament is the developed sense of the building as a whole, or the manifest abstract pattern of structure itself, interpreted. Integral ornament is simply structure-pattern made visibly articulate and seen in the building as it is seen articulate in the structure of the trees or a lily of the fields. It is the expression of inner rhythm of form. Are we talking about style? Pretty nearly. At any rate, we are talking about the qualities that make essential architecture as distinguished from any mere act of building whatsoever.

1932a

Opposite: sketch for "The City by the Sea" mural in
Midway Gardens, Chicago, Ill., 1914

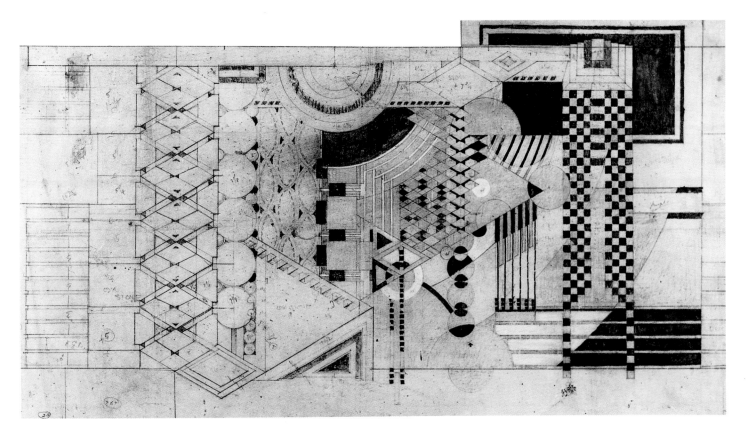

Drawing for stone panel, carved and polychromed,
in the Imperial Hotel, Tokyo, Japan, 1915-22

T square and triangle design, "December,"
one of a series of twelve months designed ca. 1933

What they now call non-objective art can be seen in patterns we designed for the Midway Gardens in 1912. Such as in this detail of a mural called "City by the Sea". But I had been making such abstract designs for fifteen years. This principle of design was natural, inevitable for me. Whether in glass or textile or whatever, it is based on the straight-line technique of the T square and the triangle. It was inherent in the Froebel system of kindergarten training given me by my mother—for I built many designs and buildings on the kitchen table out of the geometric forms of those playthings. Out of this came the straight-line patterns that are used today in textiles, linoleums and so on. But it grew out of my own limitations, by way of the T square and the triangle and the compass.

1953a

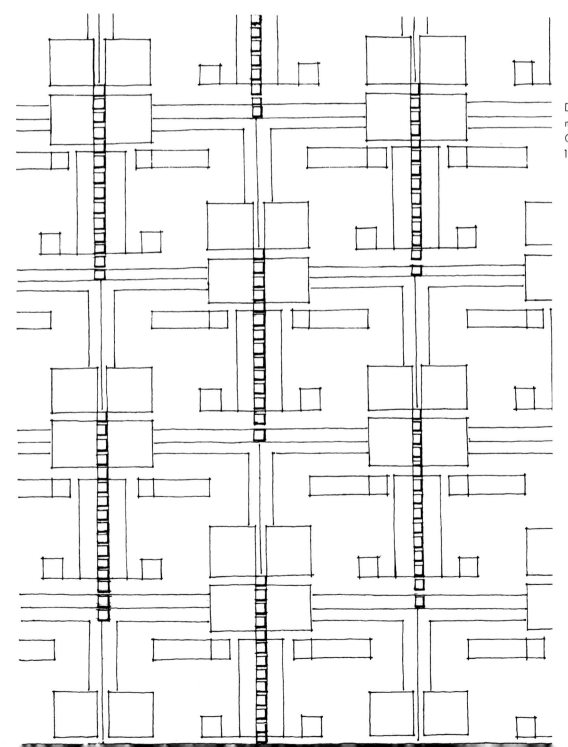

Design of exterior wall ornament, ceramic inlaid in stucco, Coonley house, Riverside, Ill., 1908

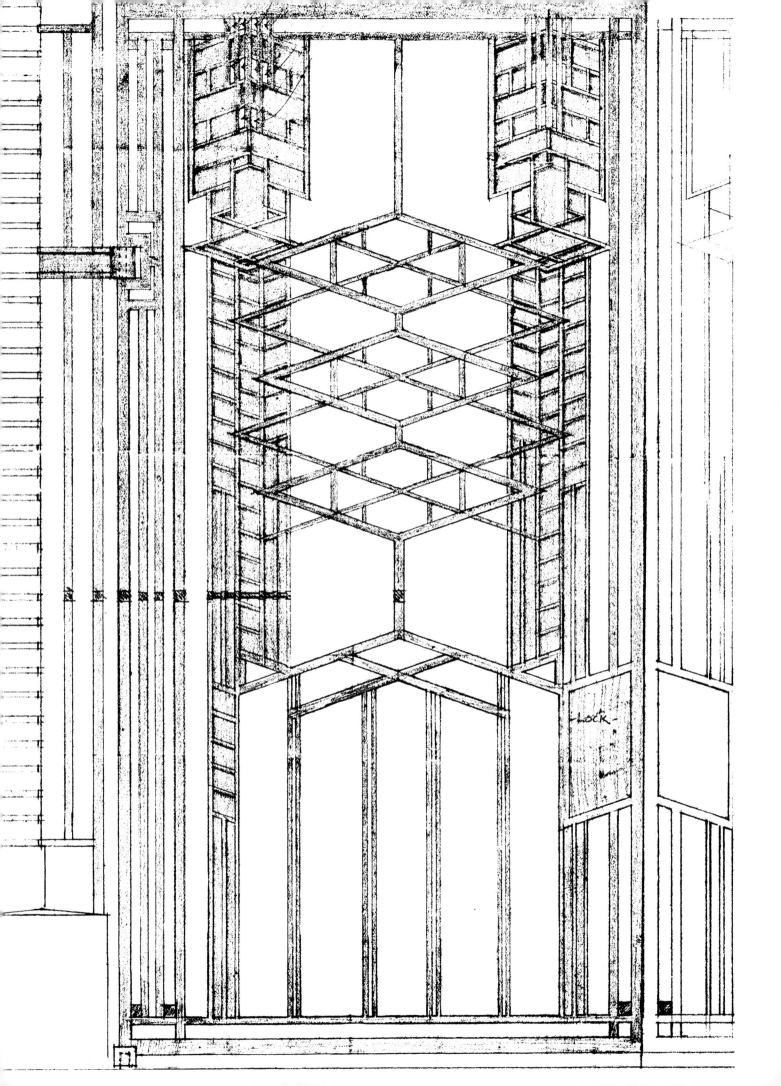

LOCK

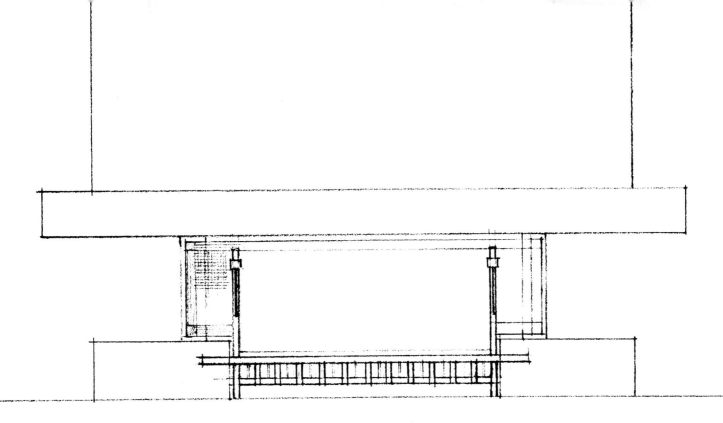

"I had been making such abstract designs for fifteen years"
Sketch for fireplace, Francis Little house, Wayzata, Minn., 1913

Sketches for windows, Coonley playhouse, Riverside,
Ill., 1912

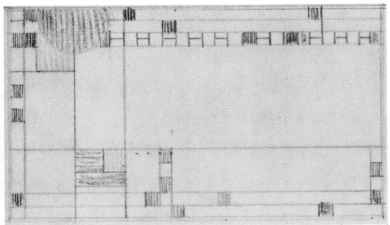

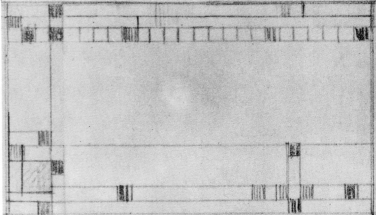

Opposite: sketch for garage gates,
Robie house, Chicago, Ill., 1909

"The rich encrustation of the shells"
Freeman house, Los Angeles, Cal., 1924

The shell as human habitation. Why not? Another phase of architecture organic. The straight line, the flat plane, now textured. The sense of interior space coming through, the openings all woven together as integral features of the shell. The rich encrustation of the shells should be visible as mass, the true mass of the architecture. Here ornament would become a legitimate feature of construction.

1932a

... To get from some native plant an expression of its native character in terms of imperishable stone to be fitted perfectly to its place in structure, and without loss of vital significance, is one great phase of great art. It means that Greek or Egyptian found a revelation of the inmost life and character of the lotus and acanthus in terms of lotus or acanthus life. That was what happened when the art of these people had done with the plants they most loved. This imaginative process is known only to the creative artist. Conventionalization, it is called. Really it is the dramatizing of an object—truest drama. To enlarge upon this simple figure, as an artist, it seems to me that this complex matter of civilization is itself at bottom some such conventionalizing process, or must be so to be successful and endure.

1931b

"Conventionalization"
Hollyhock House,
Hollywood, Cal., 1917-20

Terminal masses are most important as to form. Nature will show this to you in her own fabrications. Take good care of the terminals and the rest will take care of itself.

1928a

Hanna house, Palo Alto, Cal., 1937

WHERE PRINCIPLE IS PUT TO WORK

THERE WILL ALWAYS BE STYLE: II

FROM STRUCTURE COMES FORM AND STYLE

Form, and such style as it may own, comes out of structure — industrial, social, architectural.

Principles of construction employing suitable materials for the definite purposes of industry or society, in living hands, will result in style. The changing methods and materials of a changing life should keep the road open for developing variety 1932c of expression, spontaneous so long as human imagination lives.

Always the desire to get some system of building construction as a basis for architecture was my objective—my hope. There never was, there is no architecture otherwise, I believe.

What form? Well, let the form come. Form would come in time if a sensible, 1932a feasible system of building construction would only come first.

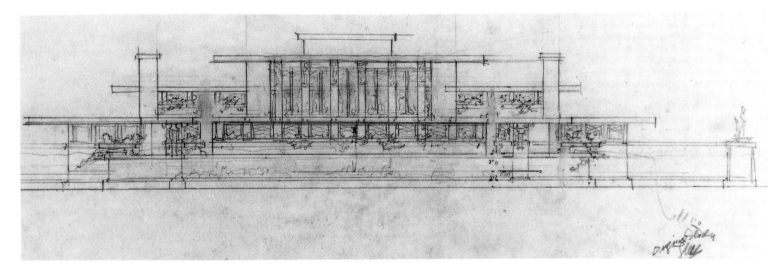

Pencil study for Coonley playhouse, Riverside, Ill., 1911

Do you think that, as a style, any aesthetic formula forced upon this work of ours in our country can do more than stultify this reasonable hope for a life of the soul?

A creative architecture for America can only mean an architecture for the 1932c individual.

"Always the desire to get some system of building construction as a basis for architecture was my objective"
Brick construction, C. R. Wall house, Plymouth, Mich., 1941

Left, structural detail used throughout; right, exterior: Auldbrass Plantation near Yemassee, S. C., 1940

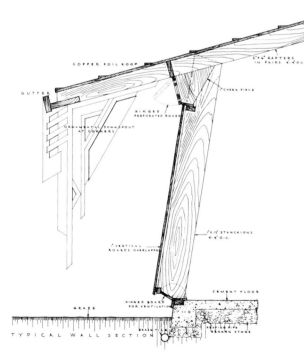

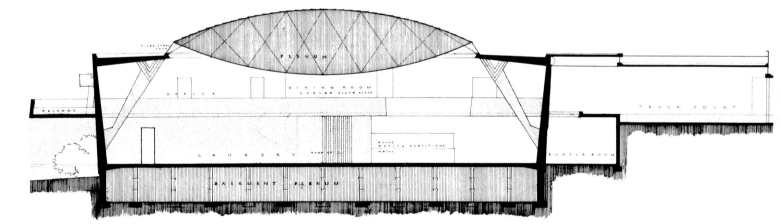

"Aesthetic and structure become completely one"
Above, perspective; below, section through building:
project for Adelman laundry, Milwaukee, Wis., 1948

But were the full import of continuity in architecture to be grasped, aesthetic and structure become completely one, it would continue to revolutionize . . . our machine-age architecture, making it superior in harmony and beauty to any architecture, Gothic or Greek. This ideal at work upon materials by nature of the process or tools used, means a living architecture in a new age, organic architecture, the only architecture that can live and let live because it never can become a mere style. Nor can it ever become a formula for the tyro. Where principle is put to work, not as a recipe or as a formula, there will always be *style* and no need to bury it 1936a as "a style."

233

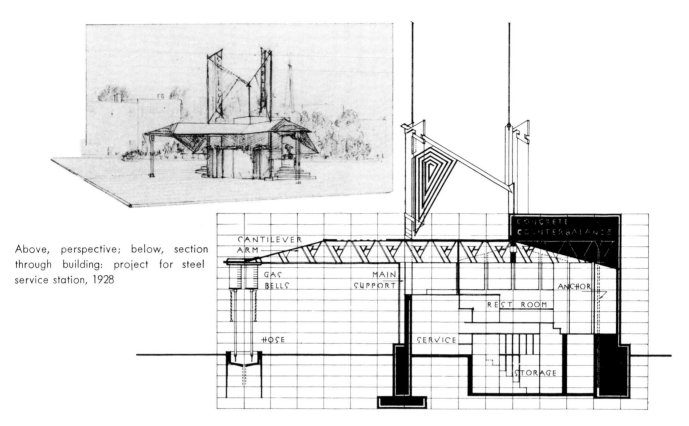

Above, perspective; below, section through building: project for steel service station, 1928

For the instance in hand, a steel building won't look like a masonry building. In the purpose of the structure itself, in the way it is built, and in what makes it stand there where it is: modern architecture is found and developed into an outside.

1931d

Now for proportion — for the concrete expression of concrete in this natural arrangement—the ideal of an organic whole well in mind. And we have arrived at the question of style. For observe: so far what has actually taken place is only reasoned arrangement; the plan kept in mind with an eye to an exterior but meantime felt, in imagination, as a whole.

1932a

Mass machine-production needs a conscience but needs no aesthetic formula as a short cut to any style; it is itself a deadly formula. Machinery needs the creative force that can seize it, as it is, for what it is worth, to get the work of the world done by it and gradually make that work no less an expression of the spontaneous human spirit than ever work was before.

1932c

Project for house spanning a ravine, Doheny ranch, California, 1921

Standardization is a mere but indispensable tool; a tool to be used only to a certain extent in all matters not purely technical or commercial or mere matters of method. Standardization is only a means to an end.

Used so that it leaves the spirit free to destroy the static element in the will; on suspicion maybe; used so only that it does not become a style, or inflexible rule, only to that extent is it desirable to the architect.

To the extent that it remains a servant of new forms or the new sense of inherent style, it is desirable.

1928b Standardization should be put to work but never allowed to master the process that yields the original form.

Blocks awaiting use, Storer house, Los Angeles, Cal., 1928

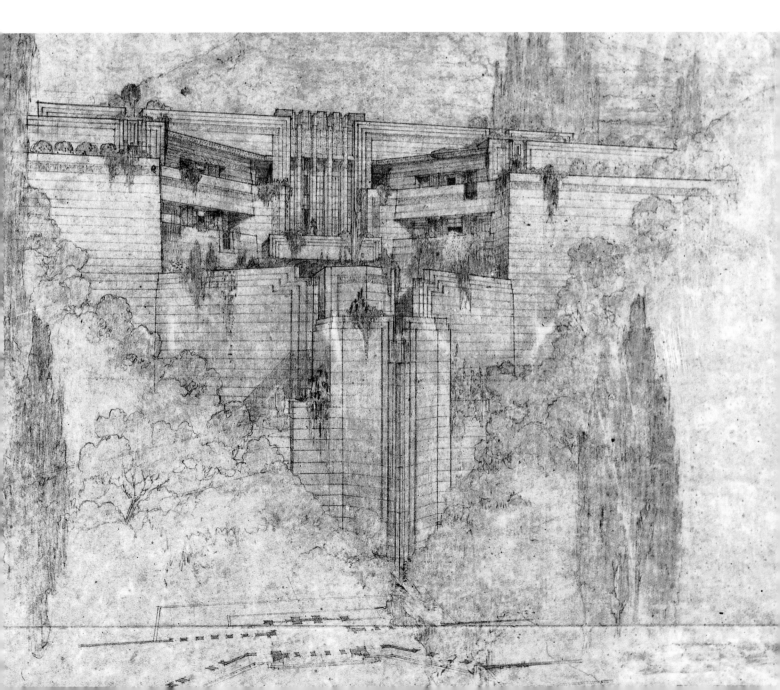

"Standardization should be put to work but never allowed to master the process that yields the original form"
Above: R. Ll. Jones house, Tulsa, Okla., 1929
Below: Entrance to La Miniatura, Pasadena, Cal., 1923

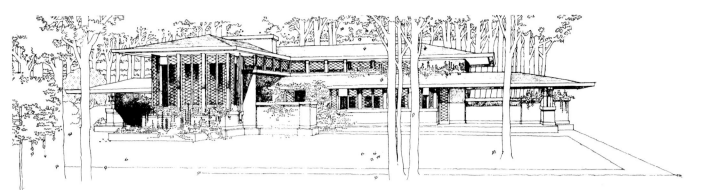

THE CHARACTERISTIC IN ARCHITECTURE

To Europeans these buildings may, on paper, seem uninhabitable; but they derive air and dignity by quite other means than excess height and all respect one ancient tradition at least—the only one here worthy of respect—the good ground itself.

The differentiation of a single, simple form characterizes the expression of any one building. Quite a different one may serve another. But, from one basic idea all form or formal elements of design are in each case derived and held firmly together in human scale and appropriate character. The form chosen may flare outward, opening flowerlike to the sky; another, droop to accentuate artistically the weight of the masses; another be noncommittal or abruptly emphatic. Or, grammar may be deduced from some plant form that has appealed to me, as certain properties in line and form of the sumac were used in the Lawrence house at Springfield. But *in every case* the motif is adhered to throughout the building.

The buildings themselves, in the sense of the whole, lack neither richness nor incident. But these qualities are secured not by applied decoration. They are found in the fashioning of the whole in which color, too, plays as significant a part as it does in an old Japanese wood block print.

These ideals when put into practice take buildings out of school and marry them to the ground; make them all intimate expressions (or revelations) of interiors and individualize them regardless of preconceived notions of Style. I have tried to make their grammar perfect in its way and to give their forms and proportions integrity that will bear study although few of them can be intelligently studied apart from environment.

1910a

"I have tried to make their grammar perfect . . . to give their forms and proportions integrity"
Unity Church, Oak Park, Ill., 1906

"Contrast"
Cantilevers at Fallingwater, Bear Run, Pa., 1936

THE DISCIPLINE OF IDEALS

Life needs and gets interior discipline according to its ideal. The higher the ideal, the greater the discipline.

Do you know the living discipline of an ideal of life as organic architecture or architecture as organic life? Those who do know the interior discipline of this ideal look upon surrender to any style formula whatever as dead exterior discipline, imprisonment in impotence.

Well . . . if an effect is produced at all in organic architecture, it must proceed from the interior of the work. It must be of the very organism created.

Try that for discipline in our democracy!

It is an inflexible will, bridling a rich and powerful ego, that is necessary to the creation of any building as architecture or the living of any life in a free democracy. Call it individual. And it is ever so.

And any great thing is too much of whatever it is: it is a quality of greatness.

1932c   "Excess of contrast, in genius, brings about a mighty equilibrium."

Florida Southern College, Lakeland, Fla., begun 1938

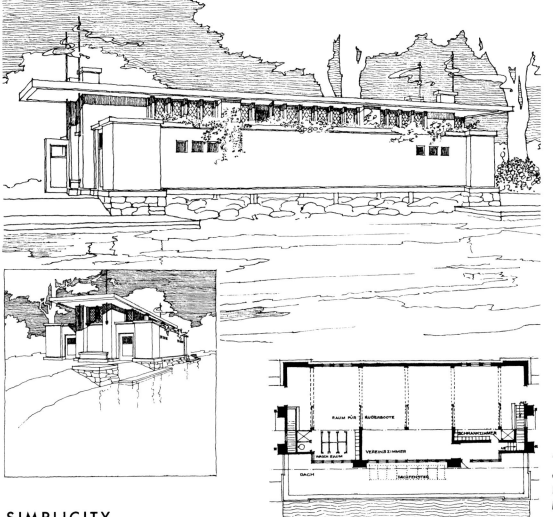

"Five lines where three are enough is always stupidity" Project for boathouse on Lake Mendota, Madison, Wis., 1902

SIMPLICITY

Five lines where three are enough is always stupidity. Nine pounds where three are sufficient is obesity. But to eliminate expressive words in speaking or writing—words that intensify or vivify meaning—is not simplicity. Nor is similar elimination in architecture simplicity. It may be, and usually is, stupidity.

In architecture, expressive changes of surface, emphasis of line and especially textures of material or imaginative pattern, may go to make facts more eloquent—forms more significant. Elimination, therefore, may be just as meaningless as elaboration, perhaps more often is so. To know what to leave out and what to put in; just where and just how, ah, that is to have been educated in knowledge of simplicity—toward ultimate freedom of expression.

This is, I believe, the single secret of simplicity: that we may truly regard nothing at all as simple in itself. I believe that no one thing in itself is ever so, but must achieve simplicity—as an artist should use the term—as a perfectly realized part of some organic whole. Only as a feature or any part becomes harmonious element in the harmonious whole does it arrive at the state of simplicity. Any wild flower is truly simple but double the same wild flower by cultivation and it ceases to be so. The scheme of the original is no longer clear. Clarity of design and perfect significance both are first essentials of the spontaneous-born simplicity of the lilies of the field. "They toil not, neither do they spin," Jesus wrote the supreme essay on simplicity in this.

1932a

Do not think that simplicity means something like the side of a barn, but rather something with graceful sense of beauty in its utility from which discord and all that is meaningless has been eliminated.

1894a

Would you have again the general principles of the spiritual ideal of organic simplicity at work in our culture? If so, then let us reiterate: first, simplicity is constitutional order. And it is worthy of note in this connection that 9×9 equals 81 is just as simple as 2×2 equals 4. Nor is the obvious more simple necessarily than the occult. The obvious is obvious simply because it falls within our special horizon, is therefore easier for us to *see;* that is all. Yet all simplicity near or far has a countenance, a visage, that is characteristic. But this countenance is visible only to those who can grasp the whole and enjoy the significance of the minor part, as such, in relation to the whole when in flower. This for the critics.

"The single secret of simplicity . . . only as a feature or any part becomes harmonious element in the harmonious whole does it arrive at the state of simplicity"

Projected residence for H. F. McCormick, Lake Forest, Ill., 1907

243

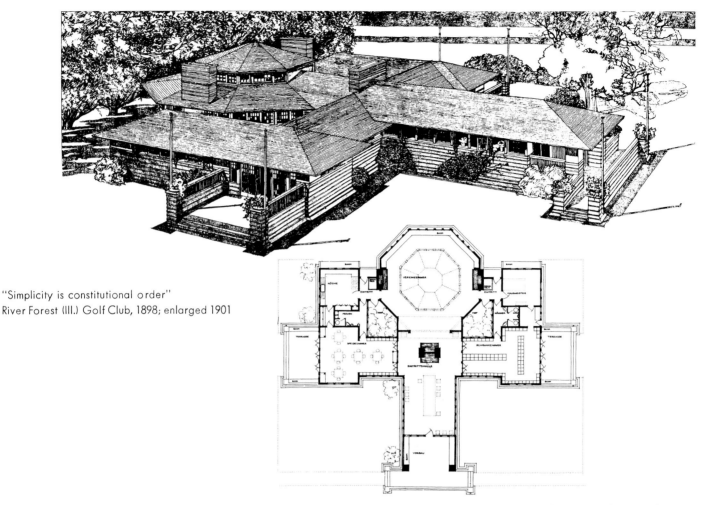

"Simplicity is constitutional order"
River Forest (Ill.) Golf Club, 1898; enlarged 1901

Truly ordered simplicity in the hands of the great artist may flower into a bewildering profusion, exquisitely exuberant, and render all more clear than ever. Good William Blake says exuberance is *beauty,* meaning that it is so in this very sense. This for the modern artist with the machine in his hands.

False simplicity—simplicity as an affectation, that is, simplicity constructed as a decorator's *outside* put upon a complicated, wasteful engineer's or carpenter's structure, outside or inside—is not good enough simplicity. It cannot be simple at all. But that is what passes for simplicity, now that startling simplicity-effects are becoming the fashion. That kind of simplicity is *violent.* This for art-and-decoration. 1931b

The first feeling therefore is for a new simplicity, a new idea of simplicity as organic. Organic simplicity might be seen producing significant character in the harmonious order we call nature: all around, beauty in growing things. None insignificant. 1931c

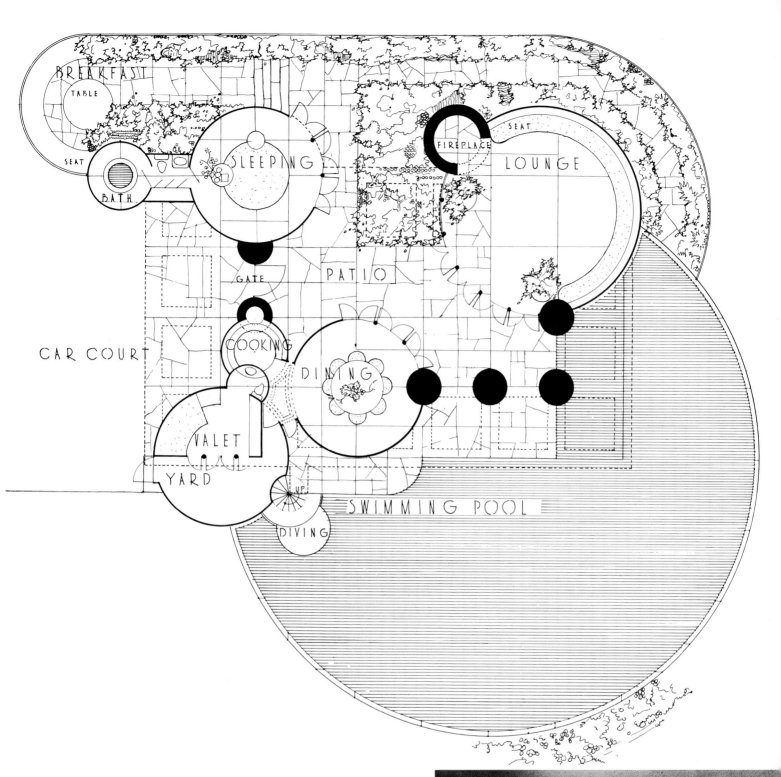

BREAKFAST

TABLE

SEAT

BATH

SLEEPING

FIREPLACE

SEAT

LOUNGE

GATE

PATIO

CAR COURT

COOKING

DINING

VALET

YARD

UP

DIVING

SWIMMING POOL

"Exuberance is beauty"
Above, plan; below, model: project for Ralph Jester, Palos
Verdes, Cal., 1938

PRINCIPLE AT WORK IN JAPAN

Becoming more closely acquainted with things Japanese, I saw the native home in Japan as a supreme study in elimination—not only of dirt but the elimination of the insignificant. So the Japanese house naturally fascinated me and I would spend hours taking it all to pieces and putting it together again. I saw nothing meaningless in the Japanese home and could find very little added in the way of ornament because all ornament as we call it, they get out of the way the necessary things are done or by bringing out and polishing the beauty of the simple materials they used in making the building. Again, you see, a kind of cleanliness.

At last I had found one country on earth where simplicity, as natural, is supreme. The floors of these Japanese homes are all made to live on—to sleep on and eat from, to kneel upon soft silken mats and meditate upon. On which to play the flute, or to make love.

Nothing is allowed to stand long as a fixture upon the sacred floors of any Japanese home. Everything the family uses is designed to be removed when not in use and be carefully put in its proper place. It is so designed and made. Beautiful to use only when appropriate and use only at the right moment. Even the partitions dividing the floor spaces are made removable for cleaning.

And strangely enough, I found this ancient Japanese dwelling to be a perfect example of the modern standardizing I had myself been working out. The floor mats, removable for cleaning, are all three feet by six feet. The size and shape of all the houses are both determined by these mats. The sliding partitions all occur at the unit lines of the mats. And they all speak of a nine, sixteen or thirty-six mat house, as the case may be.

The simple square, polished wooden posts that support the ceilings and roof, all stand at the intersections of the mats. The sliding paper shoji, or outside screens that serve in place of walls and windows to enclose interior room spaces, all slide back into recesses in the walls. Shoji are removable too. The wind blows clean beneath the floors. The sloping tiled roofs are padded with clay under heavy curved roof tiles and above beautiful, low, flat, broad-boarded ceilings to make a cool overhead. The benjo or earth-closet is usually made on one side of the garden and set well away from the "devil's corner." And as if to prove that nearly every superstition has a basis of sense, I found that corner to be the one from which the prevailing breezes blow. Semi-detached from the house, the benjo is reached under shelter on polished plank floors. Beside it stands always a soft-water cistern, perhaps made of some hollowed-out natural stone or a picturesque garden feature made or set up out of various natural stones. Or it may be a great bronze bowl brimming with water. A delicate little bamboo dipper lies across the pool of water to be lifted by the little housemaid who will pour clean water over the hands of the master or of his guests as either leaves the benjo. Another libation to the Shinto god of cleanliness. A little confusing at first perhaps to the foreign guest, and no little embarrassment.

And the kitchen? Go down several steps to find that, for it is tiled flat with the ground and also goes high up into the rafters for ventilation. It is like a cool, clean, well-ventilated studio. Its simple appointments are of hand-polished concrete or fine hard stone. The kitchen is hung with a collection of copper kettles and lacquerware that would drive a Western collector quite off his head, and has.

But the bathroom! This holy of holies is a good-sized detached pavilion, too, again flush with the ground and floored over with stone or tiles so pitched that water thrown from a bucket will drain away. Over the stone floor is a slat floor of wood on which to stand in bare feet, the water going through freely. The built-in wooden tub is square and deep, made to stand up in. It is always heated from beneath.

As with every native, so I have often been soaped and scrubbed before I was allowed to be tubbed. After that only might I step in and cook the germs off me. To any extent I was able to stand up to. Yes, that Shinto bath is a fine and religious thing, but so is everything else about the establishment. And bathing is perpetual. It has been made easy. The Japanese man or woman may loosen only the girdle and the garments all slip off together in one gesture. They put them all on again the same simple easy way. In their costume too, see simplicity, convenience, repose—their bodies as easily kept clean as their houses. Shinto made it and will have it so. I found it wholly convenient and I wore the native costume whenever in a Japanese inn or dwelling. And much impressed the native inns.

For pleasure in all this human affair you couldn't tell where the garden leaves off and the garden begins. I soon ceased to try, too delighted with the problem to

248

solve it. There are some things so perfect that nothing justifies such curiosity.

By heaven, here was a house used by those who made it with just that naturalness with which a turtle uses his shell. It is as like the natives as the polished bronze of their skin, the texture of their polished hair or the look in their slant and sloe eyes.

We of the West couldn't live in Japanese houses and we shouldn't. But we could live in houses disciplined by an ideal at least as high and fine as this one of theirs —if we went about it for a half century or so. I am sure the West needs this source of inspiration. For once, it can't very well copy. The ethnic eccentricity is too great. The West can copy nearly everything easier than it can copy the Japanese house or Japanese things for domestic uses.

1932a

Interior, old Shoin, Katsura Villa, ca. 1600

THE FUTURE OF ORGANIC ARCHITECTURE

FORECAST

I declare, the time is here for architecture to recognize its own nature, to realize the fact that it is out of life itself for life as it is now lived, a humane and therefore an intensely human thing; it must again become the most human of all the expressions of human nature. Architecture is a necessary interpretation of such human life as we now know if we ourselves are to live with individuality and beauty.

Out of the ground into the light—yes! Not only must the building so proceed, but we cannot have an organic architecture unless we achieve an organic society! We may build some buildings for a few people knowing the significance or value of that sense of the whole which we are learning to call organic, but we cannot have an architecture for a society such as ours now is. We who love architecture and recognize it as the great sense of structure in whatever is—music, painting, sculpture, or life itself—we must somehow act as intermediaries—maybe missionaries.

1939a

Aerial view, project for Bailleres house, Acapulco, Mexico, 1952

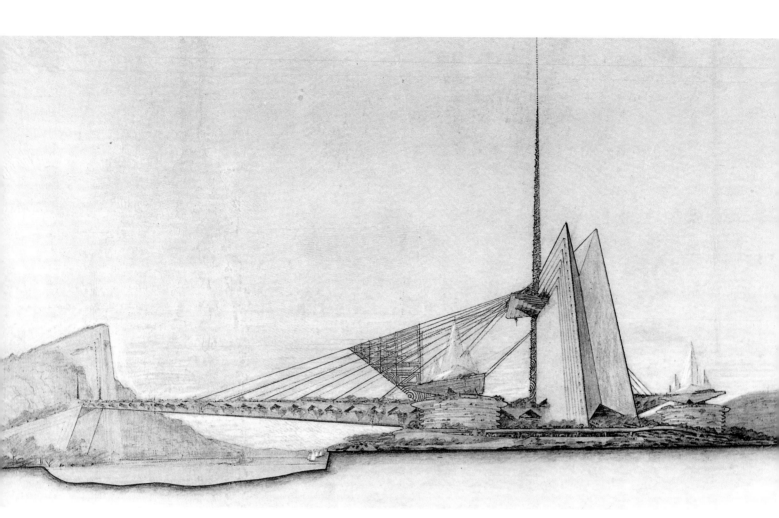

South side of project for twin suspension bridges at Point Park, Pittsburgh, Pa., 1947

Mankind is only now waking to any vision of the machine as the true emancipator of the individual as an individual. Therefore we may yet see the machine age as the age of a true democracy, wherein human life is based squarely on and in the beauty and fruitfulness of the ground: life lived in the full enjoyment of the earthline of human life—the line of freedom for man. Man's horizon may be immeasurably extended by the machine, the creature of his brain at the service of his heart and mind.

1931c

The machine, once our formidable adversary, is ready and competent to undertake the drudgeries of living on this earth. The margin of leisure even now widens as the machine succeeds. This margin of leisure should be spent with the fields, in the gardens; and in travel. The margin should be expanded and devoted to making beautiful the environment in which human beings are born to live—into which one brings the children who will be the Usonia of tomorrow.

1931b

We now have reasonably safe mechanical means to build buildings as tall as we want to see them, and there are many places and uses for them in any village, town, or city, but especially in the country. Were we to learn to limit such buildings to their proper places and give them the integrity as standardized steel and glass and copper they deserve, we would be justly entitled to a spiritual pride in them; our submission to them would not then be servile in any sense. We might take genuine pride in them with civic integrity. The skyscraper might find infinite expression in variety—as beauty.

. . . When the mind is disciplined by this power to see in the abstract the actual patterns of nature; yes, in this case the very patterns of steel construction, the skeleton will become an important feature and, in its proper place, will not be paraded as a discovery for its own sake. The skeleton is a novelty just now. Architects are discovering that bones have picturesque effects. To skin the bones is, therefore, an architectural pursuit at the present moment.

But the method of creation is still to come in this effort with steel.

Only as the principle of construction; cantilever, hanger, post, or beam, does steel find expression in natural pattern (yes, all these elements of architecture have their creative pattern) and not until that natural pattern becomes a plastic, rhythmic fabric adapted to human needs with complete repose, not until then, I say,
1928h will this . . . result in architecture.

Project for Bailleres house, Acapulco, Mexico, 1952

253

In all modern...architecture, awakening, you see this age of the machine more freely declaring for freedom to express the simple facts of structure. Malformations of material, misuse of tools and utensils grow less.

In the new uses of these new, valid economic standards in architecture...you may see and measure the cure for the causes of urban decay. Urban decay may be a real service rendered twentieth-century mankind by the machine.

Up to and including the nineteenth century, mechanical forces did place a premium upon centralization. None the less, twentieth-century mobilizations—electrifications in multiple forms—are advance agents of decentralization and a fresh integration.

It is not so difficult to see now that man has only to get this monster, the machine, into the service of his trained imagination and get machine-increment where it belongs—into the hands of his better self—then the big city becomes a survival fit only for burial: dead; the natural consequence of that grand mechanical success which, today, is only a form of human excess. A finer ideal of machine age luxury as primarily human is coming out of, or coming along with, our modern architecture today.

Project for self-service garage on spiral concrete ramps, Pittsburgh, Pa., 1947

1932a

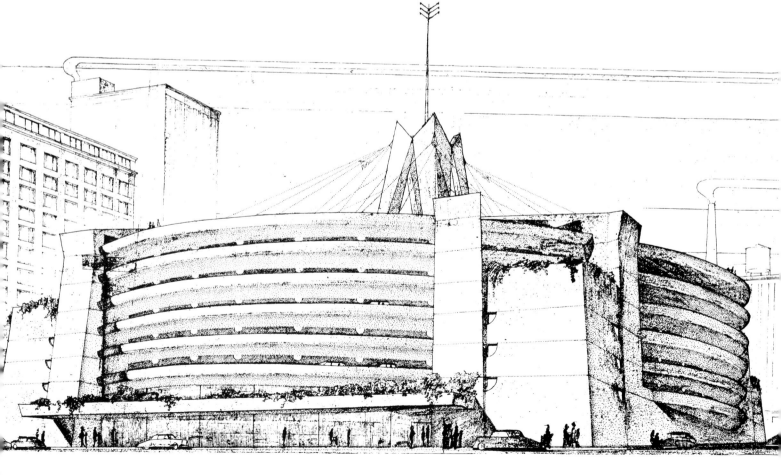

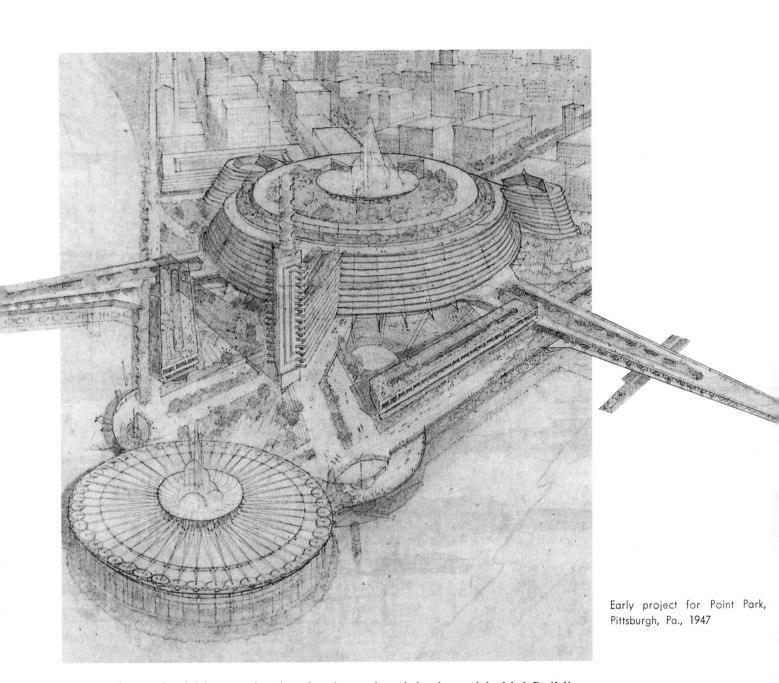

Early project for Point Park,
Pittsburgh, Pa., 1947

Imagine a city iridescent by day, luminous by night, imperishable! Buildings, shimmering fabrics, woven of rich glass; glass all clear or part opaque and part clear, patterned in color or stamped to harmonize with the metal tracery that is to hold all together, the metal tracery to be, in itself, a thing of delicate beauty consistent with slender steel construction, expressing the nature of that construction in the mathematics of structure, which are the mathematics of music as well. Such a city would clean itself in the rain, would know no fire alarms; no, nor any glooms.

To any extent the light could be reduced within the rooms by screens, blinds, or insertion of translucent or opaque glass. The heating problem would be no greater than with the rattling windows of the imitation masonry structure, because the fabric now would be mechanically perfect, the product of the machine shop instead of the makeshift of the topsy-turvy field. And the glass area would be increased only by about 10 percent over such buildings as they still continue to build of masonry.

I dream of such a city. I have worked enough on such a building to see definitely its desirability and its practicability.

1928c

What the American people have to learn is that architecture is the great mother art, the art behind which all the others are definitely, distinctly and inevitably related. Until the time comes that when we speak of art we immediately think of buildings, we will have no culture of our own.

1953a

When *unfolding* architecture as distinguished from *enfolding* architecture comes to America there will be truth of feature related to truth of being: individuality realized as a noble attribute of *being. That* is the character the architecture of democracy will take, and probably that architecture will be an expression of the highest form of aristocracy the world has conceived when we analyze it.

1931b

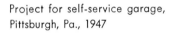

Project for self-service garage, Pittsburgh, Pa., 1947

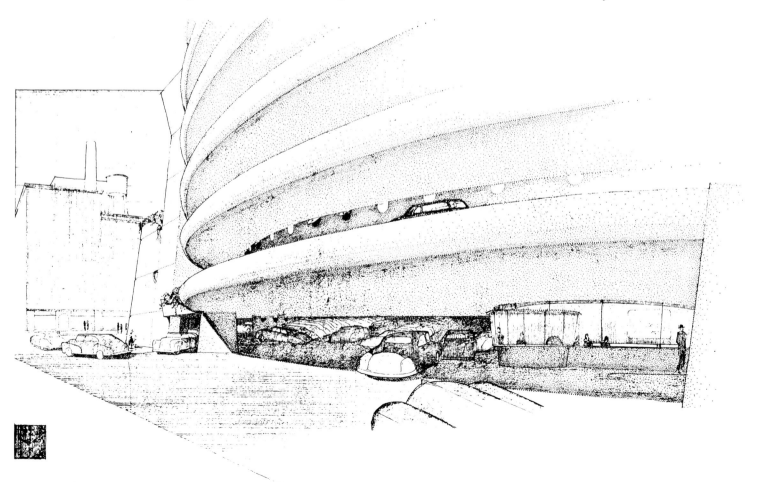

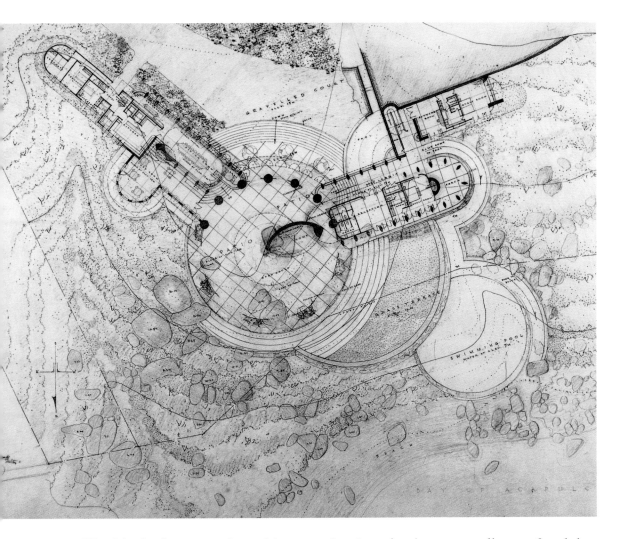

The ideal of an organic architecture for America is no mere license for doing the thing that you please to do as you please to do it in order to hold up the strange thing when done with the "see what I have made" of childish pride. Nor is it achieved by speaking the fancied language of form and function; cant terms learned by rote; or prating foolishly of progress before precedent; that unthinking, unthinkable thing! In fact, it is precisely the total absence of any conception of this ideal standard that is made conspicuous by this folly and the practices that go with it.

1914a

In time, safe inner discipline has come to me: the interior discipline of a great ideal. There is none so severe. But no other discipline yields such rich rewards in work, nor is there any man so safe and sure of results as the man disciplined from within by this ideal of the integration that is organic. Experience is this man's school. It is yet his only school.

1936a

TO THE YOUNG MAN IN ARCHITECTURE

Do not try to teach design. Teach principles.

1936a

You ask what I would advise a young man going into architecture? Well, in my new book there is a lecture I gave in Chicago in 1931 and these are the things I told him concerning ways and means:

To forget the architectures of the world except as something good in their way and in their time; not to go into architecture to get a living unless he loved it as a principle at work; to beware of architectural school except as an exponent of engineering; to go into the field to see the machines and methods at work that make modern buildings.

I said he should immediately form the habit of thinking "why" concerning effects, challenge every feature, learn to distinguish the curious from the beautiful and get the habit of analysis.

I told him to "think in simples" as my old master used to say, meaning to reduce the whole to its parts. And to abandon as poison the American idea of the quick turnover, to avoid getting into practice half-baked and to take time to prepare—even ten years.

The physician can bury his mistakes, but the architect can only advise his client to plant vines—so he should go as far as possible from home to build his first buildings. I said also to regard it just as desirable to build a chicken house as a cathedral—quality is what counts. And to stay out of architectural competitions, except as a novice and to beware of the shopper for plans. In architecture the job should find the man. And to keep his own ideal of honesty so high that he would never quite be able to reach it.

1953a

Sketch for vast interfaith steel cathedral, 1926

You must read the book of nature. What we must know in organic architecture is not found in books. It is necessary to have recourse to Nature with a capital N in order to get an education. Necessary to learn from trees, flowers, shells—objects which contain truths of form following function. If we stopped there, then it would be merely imitation. But if we dig deep enough to read the principles upon which these are activated, we arrive at secrets of form related to purpose that would make of the tree a building and of the building a tree.   1953a

My father—a preacher and a minister—taught me to regard a symphony as an edifice of sound. And ever since, as I listen to Bach and Beethoven and Mozart, I have watched the builder build and learned many valuable things from music, another phase of understanding nature.   1953a

Project for Bailleres house,
Acapulco, Mexico, 1952

And as a preparation for organic architecture a knowledge derived from nature, not only observation but constant association with the elements of nature—well,
1953a these are the basis of an architectural education.

The workings of principle in the direction of integral order is your only safe
1931c precedent, now or ever.

I am here to assure you that the circumference of architecture is changing with
1931c astonishing rapidity but that its center remains unchanged, the human heart.

261

Project for twin suspension bridges at Point Park, Pittsburgh, Pa., 1947

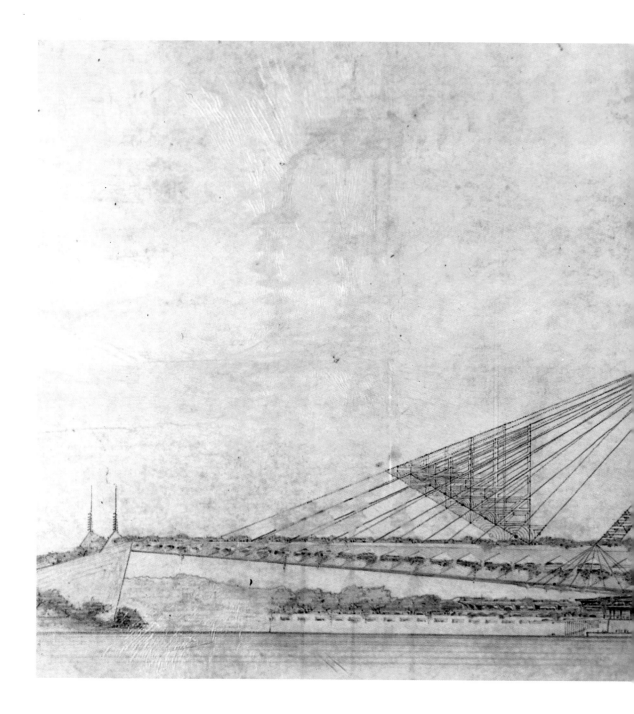

SOURCE LIST and ACKNOWLEDGMENTS

EDITOR'S NOTE: No one could undertake a book such as this without consulting and benefiting by that excellent anthology *On Architecture,* containing quotations from Frank Lloyd Wright's publications, speeches and manuscripts, edited by Frederick Gutheim and published in 1941 by Duell, Sloan & Pearce.

1894

    a. To the University Guild, Evanston, Ill.

1896

    a. To the University Guild, Evanston, Ill.

1902

    a. To the Chicago Women's Club

1908

    a. *The Architectural Record,* March

1910

    a. *Sovereignty of the Individual,* originally written and published as the text of *Ausgführte Bauten und Entwürfe.* Berlin: Wasmuth

1914

    a. *The Architectural Record,* May

1928

    The Architectural Record:
        a. January
        b. February
        c. April
        d. May
        e. July
        f. August
        g. October
        h. Taliesin files

1929

    a. *The Architectural Record,* July
    b. Taliesin files

1930

    a. *The Architectural Forum,* May
    b. Taliesin files

1931

    a. To the Michigan Society of Architects, and Grand Rapids Chapter, American Institute of Architects
    b. *Modern Architecture* (The Kahn Lectures). Princeton: Princeton University Press
    c. *Two Lectures on Architecture.* The Art Institute of Chicago
    d. Taliesin files

1932

    a. *An Autobiography:* 1st edition. New York: Longmans, Green & Co.; see Note following Source List
    b. *Saturday Review of Literature,* May 21
    c. *Shelter,* April
    d. *Wisconsin Magazine*
    e. Taliesin files

1935

    a. *Taliesin.* An occasional publication of the Taliesin Fellowship

1936

    a. *Architect's Journal* of London, "Recollections. The United States: 1893-1920," July 16-August 6. Permission gratefully acknowledged

1936-1940

    a. *Capitol Times,* Madison, Wisconsin

1937

    a. *Architecture and Modern Life,* by Baker Brownell and Frank Lloyd Wright. New York: Harper & Brothers. Permission gratefully acknowledged
    b. Answers to questions by *Architecture of U.S.S.R.*
    c. Taliesin files

1938

    a. *The Architectural Forum,* January
    b. To the Association of Federal Architects

1939

    a. *An Organic Architecture: The Architecture of Democracy.* London: Lund Humphries & Co., Ltd. (the "London Lectures")

1940

a. *Arizona Highways,* May

1943

a. *An Autobiography,* 2nd edition. New York: Duell, Sloan & Pearce; see Note following Source List

1949

a. *The New Theatre,* catalog of the Wadsworth Athenaeum, Hartford, Conn.

1951

a. *The Architectural Forum,* January

1952

a. Address to the Junior Chapter of the American Institute of Architects, New York City. Taped and typed; corrected by F. Ll. W.

b. *The Architectural Forum,* April

1953

a. *New York Times Magazine,* October 4

b. Talk to Taliesin Fellowship. Taped and typed; corrected by F. Ll. W. (After this source list was completed, further research revealed that this talk was given on May 28, 1950, not 1953.)

1954

a. *The Natural House.* New York: Horizon Press

NOTE

There have been two editions of *An Autobiography* by Frank Lloyd Wright. The first was published by Longmans, Green & Co. in 1932. The second edition, considerably revised and enlarged by Mr. Wright, was published by Duell, Sloan & Pearce in 1943. All passages quoted in this book which originally appeared in the first edition are identified in the present text by the date 1932; passages which Mr. Wright added in the revised edition are identified by the date 1943. The text of all passages quoted follows Mr. Wright's revisions for the 1943 edition; it is this edition which has been used for the list of page references:

An American Architecture	*An Autobiography*	*An American Architecture*	*An Autobiography*
28	380	144-47	170 *et seq.*
31	156 *et seq.*	150-54	214 *et seq.*
31-33	156 *et seq.*	159-60	310 *et seq.*
33	156 *et seq.*	163-64	313 *et seq.*
36-37	151	164-66	472 *et seq.*
56-59	145	167-69	476 *et seq.*
61	349	173-74	490 *et seq.*
61	349	190	171
70	141 *et seq.*	190	173
71-72	143	196-98	309 *et seq.*
86	348	205	146 *et seq.*
87	344	210-11	147 *et seq.*
88	159	210-11	341 *et seq.*
92	323 *et seq.*	217	337 *et seq.*
99	345	220	346 *et seq.*
105-106	338 *et seq.*	227	235
110	234 *et seq.*	231	234
114-15	316 *et seq.*	234	156 *et seq.*
115-20	256 *et seq.*	241-42	144
126-33	253 *et seq.*	246-49	196 *et seq.*
137-38	150 *et seq.*	249	199
140-44	154 *et seq.*	254	350

PHOTOGRAPHERS' CREDITS

RICHARD CHEEK (COURTESY OF COURRIER GALLERY): 18

FUERMANN: 71, 72 (bottom)

SAMUEL H. GOTTSCHO: 169

P. E. GUERRERO: 53, 111, 112

HEDRICH-BLESSING STUDIO: 22, 56, 57, 81, 102

HOLLAND: 55, 232 (bottom right)

PHOTOGRAPHIC DEPARTMENT, S. C. JOHNSON AND SON: 35, 51 (bottom right), 83, 84, 104 (bottom), 106, 108, 125

TORKEL KORLING: 105, 124 (left)

FRED LYON: 98, 101

MC LAUGHLIN & COMPANY: 188

W. ALBERT MARTIN: 203, 236 (bottom)

P. MAYEN: 90, 91, 239

MOEN: 165 (right)

JOE MUNROE: 232 (top)

MAYNARD L. PARKER: 20

ROY E. PETERSEN: 124 (right), 166, 245 (bottom)

JOE D. PRICE: 113, 114

TATSUZO SATO: 109, 248

EZRA STOLLER: 42, 103

STURTEVANT: 214

LUKE SWANK: 82, 107

J. SZARKOWSKI: 32, 43, 238

WESTELIN: 191

MASON WEYMOUTH: 25, 28

H. S. K. YAMAGUCHI: 153 (middle), 211